CALIFORNIA
AUTO ACCIDENT
CLAIMS

CALIFORNIA
AUTO ACCIDENT
CLAIMS

A COMPREHENSIVE GUIDE

JIMIN OH

California Auto Accident Claims
Jimin Oh

ISBN Paperback: 978-1-7377018-0-4
ISBN E-book: 978-1-7377018-1-1

Legal Disclaimer

The information in this book is not legal advice. This book is solely intended to help accident victims by providing general information and tips. It does not replace hiring an attorney for specific legal advice pertaining to your case.

The laws change frequently and may be subject to different interpretations for different facts. Thus, you should contact an attorney if you have any specific questions concerning your case.

Although the author has made every effort to ensure that the information in this book was correct at the time of publishing, the author does not assume any liability to any party for any loss or damage caused by the content of this book.

Table of Contents

PART A

UNDERSTANDING YOUR AUTO ACCIDENT CLAIM

Chapter 1

What to Do After a Car Accident

Getting into a car accident can be terrifying and confusing, which can lead to you making the wrong decisions immediately after the crash.

Unfortunately, making the wrong choices can keep you from receiving the compensation that you deserve. Worse, it can leave you covering the cost of the accident — even if it wasn't your fault. Let's look at an example.

On her way to work, Kim legally drives through an intersection after the traffic light turns green. Out of nowhere, she is T-boned by a car that clearly ran a red light. On impact, Kim feels neck pain and a mild headache.

The driver of the other vehicle asks Kim, out of what seems like genuine concern, if she is alright. Kim says that she thinks she is okay.

Since the accident made Kim late for work, she agrees to just exchange information with the other driver and have the insurance companies work it out. A few witnesses approach Kim to make sure she is alright, and Kim tells them that she is fine. Because her car is still drivable, Kim leaves the scene of the accident and goes to work.

The next morning, Kim experiences neck and shoulder pain on waking. She calls her primary care physician and schedules an appointment for the first opening, which is three weeks later. At the appointment, Kim's doctor recommends six weeks of physical therapy.

Kim calls the other driver's insurance company to file a claim for the accident. She tells the adjuster what happened and asks for the insurance company to fix her car. The insurance adjuster responds with "the investigation is pending."

After waiting eight weeks, the adjuster from the insurance company finally calls Kim and tells her their decision. They determined that the other driver was not at fault. When Kim asks why, the adjuster says that there is no evidence the other driver ran the red light — no witness statements, no dashcam footage, and no police report. Due to this decision, Kim is left to foot the bill for both her car's damage and her medical bills.

To determine what Kim did wrong, you first need to understand what you should do after a car accident.

CALL THE POLICE TO FILE AN ACCIDENT REPORT

No matter how minor the accident appears at the time, you should always call the police to file a report. A police determination of who is at fault is usually very persuasive to insurance companies, and a police report can help avoid a he-said-she-said situation like Kim's.

The more confusion surrounds who is at fault, the more critical it becomes to involve the police. If the vehicle's damage does not clearly show what happened in the accident, then a police officer at the scene taking statements will strengthen your case. For example, witness statements are much more essential in a side-crash or T-bone accident than in a rear-end collision, as vehicle damage will most likely show you were hit from behind.

Sometimes, the police will ask if anyone is seriously injured when you call. If the answer is no, then law enforcement may decline to attend the scene and simply advise you to exchange information with the other driver. When this happens, it is even more critical to follow the steps in this chapter (taking photos, obtaining all the information, etc.) at the scene.

IF YOU ARE INJURED, AGREE FOR AN AMBULANCE TO TAKE YOU TO HOSPITAL

After an event like a car crash, adrenaline floods your system and can stop pain signals from telling your brain that you are seriously hurt. Adrenaline can also prevent you from understanding the true extent of your injuries — some are not immediately apparent, while other injuries may worsen over time.

If you go to hospital in an ambulance, medical personnel can observe you and provide care until a doctor can treat you. Your symptoms could also suddenly worsen, and if you attempt to drive to a hospital or somewhere else, you could put your health and other drivers in danger.

Any serious pain should require an ambulance. Some of these include:

- Back pain
- Neck pain
- Lightheadedness
- Chest pain
- Difficulty breathing
- Bleeding

You should also consider calling an ambulance if your head hit the window or airbag. If the accident was a minor fender bender, and you are entirely sure you are not seriously injured, then you can choose to drive yourself and wait to be medically evaluated.

Refusing an ambulance at the scene may damage your case's value in the long run. Later, when you or your lawyer tries to negotiate a fair settlement offer for your claim, the other party could argue that you would have called for an ambulance if you were severely injured.

Therefore, you should only refuse to take an ambulance when you are 100% positive that you are not seriously injured. If you have any doubts at all, simply call for one.

TAKE PHOTOS OF THE VEHICLES INVOLVED, THE SCENE, AND YOUR INJURIES

After the accident, take photos of the vehicles involved in the crash. This includes capturing images from all angles, close-up and far away, making sure to document all the damage. You should also take photos of the accident location and any road conditions that could have caused the crash. These pictures can be used as evidence to strengthen your case.

In a multi-vehicle crash, take photos of damages to ALL vehicles involved – not just yours and the car behind you. Take pictures of any other damaged property, such as a light pole or a highway fence.

If it's too dangerous to get out of your car and take pictures, such as the highway, then skip this step and wait for the police to arrive.

You should also photograph any injuries you sustained, including bruises, scratches, and bleeding.

OBTAIN CONTACT INFORMATION FROM THE OTHER DRIVER(S) AND WITNESSES

Ensure you always get the other driver's name, address, and phone number, as well as their driver's license number, license plate number, and insurance information. You should also try to obtain any names and phone numbers from any witnesses in case the police miss anyone while making their report.

So, let's go back to Kim's story. How could she have received a better outcome?

1. She should have called the police to the scene of the accident. A police report assigning fault to the other driver would have prevented a he-said-she-said situation.

2. She should have immediately sought medical treatment. Kim felt instant pain after the crash but did not see a doctor until three weeks later. She also told the other driver and witnesses that she was fine before driving away to work instead of immediately taking an ambulance to hospital.

3. She should have taken photos of the scene. Any photos Kim had taken at the scene could have been used as evidence that the other driver had been at fault.

4. She should have written down witness contact information. Kim should have obtained contact information from the multiple witnesses who approached her as their statements could have been used as evidence of the other driver's fault.

Don't end up like Kim. Instead, use this checklist to make sure you do everything you can to protect your right to compensation if you get into a car accident:

❑ Call the police to file an accident report
❑ Take an ambulance from the scene if you think you are injured
❑ Take photos of the vehicles involved and the scene of the crash
❑ Get contact information from the other driver and any witnesses

Chapter 2

Three Mistakes to Avoid After an Accident

Now that you know the right way to handle a car accident, let's talk about some common mistakes people make that can hurt their injury cases and limit the amount of compensation they can receive.

MISTAKE #1: GIVING RECORDED STATEMENTS TO INSURANCE COMPANIES

Never forget that insurance companies are NOT on your side. They are for-profit businesses, and part of their strategy to make more money is to pay less for every claim.

A method insurance adjusters use to undermine your claim is requesting a recorded statement about the accident. The goal is to limit their driver's responsibility and place some blame on you. Some adjusters may even intentionally try to get you to say something that will hurt your case by asking leading questions.

For example, if the adjuster casually asks you how you are and you say that you are "fine" out of habit or politeness, then they could use that as evidence to claim that your injuries are minor.

Luckily, you don't have to play their games. No matter what the other driver's insurance adjuster tries to tell you, you are NOT legally required to provide a recorded statement. If the adjuster asks or even demands that you do this, you have every right to say NO.

Your attorney, if you hire one, will handle all communication with the insurance company. A personal injury attorney experienced in dealing with car crashes knows all their tricks and will not give them any information that could hurt your claim.

If you do not have an attorney, you should agree to give the insurance company the information needed to process the claim, but make sure you refuse to provide a recorded statement.

A few tips when talking to an insurance adjuster without an attorney are:

1. Review the police report before talking to the claim adjuster.

2. Clearly explain the facts showing the other driver was at fault for the accident.

3. Do not provide any unnecessary information.

4. Tell the adjuster that you were injured in the accident—even if you think the injuries are minor. No broken bones doesn't mean you're not injured.

MISTAKE #2: DELAYING MEDICAL TREATMENT

Another mistake that accident victims frequently make is waiting to get medical treatment for their injuries. You should see a doctor right away if you are hurt in a car accident. Waiting to seek medical attention could seriously diminish your claim's value because insurance adjusters will use your delay to argue that your injuries are not as severe as you say they are.

When seeing a doctor, make sure you mention every injury you received, including any pain and discomfort, no matter how minimal. Doing this will ensure a medical record has been created for how the accident hurt you. If you don't mention an injury when you initially seek medical care, the insurance company will try to claim that you didn't receive that injury in the accident.

Some people may want to delay medical treatment for minor injuries for financial reasons. However, remember that if someone else is at fault for the accident, their insurance company will have to reimburse you for any reasonable medical expenses. Make sure you save all your medical bills and other documents relating to your medical care as evidence of your costs.

I've seen this happen time after time. Our firm receives a call from someone who got into an accident months ago and didn't seek medical treatment. Their stories are usually very similar: they didn't see a doctor because they were too busy and thought the pain would go away, but their injury worsened over time, so now they want to start treatment and receive fair compensation for their damages.

Settlement in these cases usually results in much lower amounts than for those who started treatment within a week or two after the accident.

For example, a client in a total loss accident didn't seek treatment for the first two months. She then started treatment for her constant ankle pain for about two months and received a $6,000 settlement.

Another client in a minor accident saw a doctor that same week and started physical therapy a few days later. She received a $12,000 settlement for six weeks treatment.

MISTAKE #3: ACCEPTING QUICK SETTLEMENTS FROM INSURANCE COMPANIES

The third mistake often seen when dealing with car accident insurance claims is to accept a settlement offer from the insurance company right after the accident. While it's understandable that you just want to move on with your life, an initial settlement is a lowball offer, typically well below the actual amount of compensation you are entitled to and won't come close to covering the costs of your injuries.

Just like you wouldn't pay a sticker price when buying a car, you should never accept the first settlement offer from an insurance company. Adjusters will often offer a low settlement immediately after your accident before you even know how badly you are actually injured. You'd also have to sign away your rights to any additional reimbursement. This means that you would cover the costs yourself if you rack up huge medical bills for an injury you didn't even know you had after accepting a settlement.

For example, a client got into a minor accident where he hit his front tooth on a steering wheel and needed to see a dentist. After several calls, the insurance company offered $500 compensation. The adjuster was also very rude to him, questioning him exactly how many times he hit the steering wheel and even warning him about insurance fraud.

We took his case and made sure he received all the dental treatments he needed for his chipped front tooth. After he fully recovered, the case settled at $30,000.

GET THE COMPENSATION YOU DESERVE

If you can avoid these three common mistakes that insurance companies want you to make, then you will be free to pursue full compensation for your injuries. Don't forget that everything insurance adjusters say or do could be an attempt to discredit your claim. Remember your rights, and don't let them take advantage.

Chapter 3

Damages You Can Recover from a Personal Injury Case

The compensation you are awarded for your injury is referred to as "damages" in civil lawsuits. In this chapter, we will discuss eight different types of damages you can recover through a personal injury case.

1. PROPERTY DAMAGE

In personal injury cases involving car crashes, you can receive reimbursement for any incurred costs to repair your personal property that was damaged — most obviously, your vehicle. You can also claim compensation for other items damaged during the accident, such as your cell phone, laptop, or even the clothes you wore.

You are entitled to your vehicle's actual cash value if it is considered a total loss. Under California law, total loss means the sum of the repair cost and salvage value is equal or larger than the vehicle's actual cash value.

You can also recover damages for "loss of use." In California, this amount is equal to the cost of renting a similar vehicle for how long your vehicle is out of commission. For example, if your car was in the shop for two weeks, your loss of use damages would be the cost to rent a similar car for two weeks.

These are just a few examples of property damage types. We'll talk about additional compensation you can receive for property damage in Part B: Property Damage.

2. MEDICAL EXPENSES

After a car crash, you can also recover damages for necessary and reasonable accident-related medical bills. This means that you can be compensated for the cost of diagnosing and treating any injuries the accident caused, as long as the costs are not excessive or unnecessary.

In addition, recovered damages cover any estimated future medical expenses if it is reasonably certain that you will incur these after the settlement. Your doctor should provide an estimate of your future medical expenses and the reasons for your continued treatment.

3. PAIN AND SUFFERING

You can recover damages for pain and suffering to compensate for the physical and emotional anguish the accident has caused. Pain and suffering can include physical ailments from injuries, as well as mental, emotional, and psychological traumas, such as PTSD or depression. Damage value can vary based on the circumstances of your car accident and your injury. So, someone who suffers a severe injury, such as losing a limb, would likely be entitled to far greater pain and suffering damages than someone who only had a few bumps and bruises.

You can receive compensation for both pain and suffering you have already endured and any you will endure in the future. However, under California law, driving without car insurance at the time of the accident means you are not entitled to pain and suffering damages (Proposition 213).

4. LOST WAGES

Lost wage damages can be recovered if you lose income as a direct result of an injury from the car accident. For example, if you have a job that requires you to be on your feet all day and your injury puts you in a wheelchair, you would be entitled to compensation for the amount of money you would have earned if you had been able to go to work.

5. LOSS OF EARNING CAPACITY

You are also entitled to lost earning capacity from injuries that impair your ability to earn money in the future. Your future earning potential will be calculated using your past earnings as a guide and will include the amount of money you would have reasonably earned if you had not been injured.

You can receive damages against loss of earnings if you are unable to work at all, or if you can work but your earnings have been reduced due to your injury. For example, if you used to work 40 hours a week but you can now only work 20, then you can recover the amount you would have earned for the remaining hours.

6. SCARRING AND DISFIGUREMENT

Disfiguring injuries caused by the accident can include visible scarring, broken facial bones, damage to teeth, and severe burns. Damages associated with scarring and disfigurement would include the cost of any cosmetic surgery, as well as compensation for emotional injuries such as embarrassment, humiliation, and/or social rejection.

The amount of payment you can receive depends on certain factors, such as the disfiguring injury's severity and visibility; for example, the location of a scar and whether the injury is permanent. Facial scarring generally entitles you to more compensation, since it is the most visible, followed by scars on the neck or hands.

7. PUNITIVE DAMAGES

Drivers who were drunk, high, excessively speeding, or otherwise "criminally negligent" in causing your car accident may entitle you to punitive damages. These are additional costs that are meant to punish someone for their unacceptable behavior and go above and beyond compensating you for your injuries.

8. WRONGFUL DEATH

If your family member was killed in a car crash as the result of the other driver's illegal or wrongful behavior, then you may be entitled to compensation for their wrongful death. Damages can include funeral expenses and the loss of earnings, companionship, emotional support, and others you have suffered as a result of your loved one's death.

KEEP TRACK OF YOUR DAMAGES

Following a car accident, you could be entitled to receive any of the above damages, depending on the facts of your case. It is important to keep documentation of any costs you incur from the accident, as it can be used to prove the amount of your damages.

Chapter 4

Process of a Car Accident Injury Case

In this chapter, we'll walk through the details of a typical car accident case when a client hires our personal injury law firm.

STEP #1: INITIAL MEETING

The first step in a personal injury case is an initial meeting with one of our attorneys. Our firm provides free consultations either in person or via phone. During this initial meeting, we discuss the following topics:

- What our firm can do for you
- The details of your accident
- Any injuries caused by the accident
- If hiring an attorney is the right decision for you

Not every car accident victim will benefit from hiring an attorney, so we will let you know if this is the case in your situation.

After talking about the facts of the accident, we explain the general process of a personal injury case and provide you with answers to any questions you might have. Onboarding is the next step in the process if you decide to hire our firm to represent you.

STEP #2: ONBOARDING

Our onboarding paralegal will send you a personal injury packet to review and sign. This packet contains a retainer agreement and various authorization forms that allow us to act on your behalf and perform necessary tasks for your case, such as communicating with insurance companies and doctors and collecting medical records and police reports.

Once you return the signed packet, a team of legal experts is assigned to your case. This team consists of a handling attorney, onboarding paralegal, property damage assistant, and recovery specialist.

We will need to collect some documents from you. Clients can easily upload these documents and photos through the Intake Link, or they can send them via text or email.

Our standard document checklist:

A photo of your driver's license
All photos related to the accident*
The police incident card**
Your auto insurance and health insurance information
Any statements or bills from medical providers***

*Including photos of all vehicles involved, any visible injuries, the other driver's license and auto insurance card, the scene of the accident, and so on.

**We require the police incident card to request a full report from the California Highway Patrol (CHP) or local police department.

***Including the ambulance bill, emergency room after-visit summary, and so on.

STEP #3: OPEN CLAIMS AND INVESTIGATE COVERAGE

We call insurance companies so that we can open claims and investigate applicable insurance coverage. We also send a Letter of Representation to both your and the at-fault driver's respective insurance companies. Our firm then contacts either the police department or CHP (depending on who took the report) to request a full version of the accident report.

After reviewing all the relevant information, we devise the best strategy to recover full and fair compensation for you.

STEP #4: VEHICLE REPAIR AND OTHER PROPERTY DAMAGE ISSUES

Property damage issues are generally straight-forward, so we let the insurance companies contact our clients directly regarding these. However, we become involved if you run into any problems, such as repairing your vehicle or receiving reimbursement for property damage.

We ONLY permit the insurance company to talk to you about property damage issues. We NEVER give them permission to talk to you about bodily injury claims. This is primarily because they will try to use any conversation you have to hurt your case.

STEP #5: TREATMENT

We ensure that all clients receive the treatment they need to fully recover from their accidents. If you don't have health insurance or if it doesn't cover certain treatment types, then we offer medical providers (doctors, surgeons, chiropractors, etc.) who can treat you on a lien basis. This means that you only have to pay once you receive your injury settlement.

Our number one priority is ensuring your health improves — because we know that this matters the most to you. To this end, our recovery specialist regularly contacts clients to make sure they receive any and all required treatment.

Your treatment duration will vary depending on the severity of your injury and the treatment type you need. For example, soft tissue injury treatment typically takes two to five months, whereas treatment for more serious injuries, such as broken bones or brain injury, can take three months to a year (or more).

STEP #6: COLLECTING RECORDS

Once you reach Maximum Medical Improvement (MMI), we collect all medical records and itemized billing statements from each medical provider who treated you. We also gather any documents related to wage loss, pain and suffering, and other recoverable damages.

The collection stage can take one to three months, depending on how fast the hospital and your employer sends us the requested records. Some hospitals take at least 90 days to process the record requests. All we can do during this time is wait.

STEP #7: DEMAND PACKAGE

Our attorneys thoroughly review all the relevant documents once they are received before preparing a demand packet. The packet contains exhibits and a demand letter, which includes:

Facts about the accident
Liability analysis
Injury details
Medical records summary
Total sum of all past and future medical bills
Details of pain and suffering and any wage loss
Applicable California law
Legal arguments for why we believe the case should settle at the amount we demand

The exhibits include all medical records, itemized billings, wage loss documents, and other important items proving damages.

STEP #8: NEGOTIATION

The demand packet is faxed and mailed to the at-fault driver's insurance company, whereby the insurance adjuster reviews the demand. They then call or fax us the initial offer about two to three weeks later.

The negotiation process begins at this point, which consists of multiple phone calls and written correspondence between our firm and the insurance company. Our attorneys aggressively negotiate to win a full and fair settlement for our clients. Although every case is different, it typically takes approximately two to three months to secure a top offer from the insurance company. During this time, our attorneys continually inform clients about the negotiation's status.

We discuss whether you should accept the top offer once we receive it. While our attorneys advise you on the settlement and what accepting or not accepting it could mean, the decision is ultimately yours.

STEP #9: LITIGATION

Most car accident cases settle without litigation; however, we aim to sue the other driver and take the case to court if the top offer remains low. Litigation costs are high, and it could take years to obtain a judgment or a verdict, so we carefully explain the pros and cons of litigation and advise you on what we believe is best for your case.

Beware of law firms that refuse to take cases to litigation. You want a law firm that will not give in to insurance companies and will fight for what you deserve, even if it means more time and work for them.

STEP #10: DISBURSEMENT OF SETTLEMENT

The check is be mailed to our office once the case is settled — or, in litigation cases, once a judgment or verdict is reached.

We then distribute the money to you, plus the medical providers who treated you on a lien-basis, health insurance companies that paid for your accident-related medical bills, and our law firm. Our office negotiates to reduce the amount owed to medical providers and health insurance companies to maximize your share of the settlement.

IN SUMMARY

STEP #1: INITIAL MEETING

A free consultation about your case to discuss the facts of your accident and how our law firm can help you.

STEP #2: ONBOARDING

You sign paperwork, and we collect certain documents from you.

STEP #3: OPEN CLAIMS AND INVESTIGATE COVERAGE

We send a Letter of Representation to the insurance companies, request the full police report, and meet internally to strategize about your case.

STEP #4: VEHICLE REPAIR AND OTHER PROPERTY DAMAGE ISSUES

You will typically be able to handle your property damage claim yourself, but we step in if the insurance company gives you any trouble.

STEP #5: TREATMENT

Our recovery specialist ensures you get all relevant treatment and, if necessary, find medical professionals to treat you on a lien basis.

STEP #6: COLLECTING RECORDS

Once you reach MMI, we collect your medical records and bills, as well as any other documents that help prove damages.

STEP #7: DEMAND PACKAGE

We send a demand letter to the insurance company stating and justifying the amount of compensation you should receive.

STEP #8: NEGOTIATION

We negotiate with the insurance companies until we secure a top offer.

STEP #9: LITIGATION

We aim to sue the other driver and take the case to court if the top offer is too low.

STEP #10: DISBURSEMENT OF SETTLEMENT

We distribute the money to you and your creditors once the case is settled or a verdict is received.

Chapter 5

Value of the Case

Now that you know the process of a typical injury case, let's answer the question you've probably been wondering from the beginning: how much is your case worth?

Unfortunately, I can't give you a definite answer in this book as each personal injury case involves a unique set of factors affecting the final settlement. However, I can explain how the value of your case will be determined.

Four factors contribute to your case's value:
1. Liability
2. Injury severity and type
3. Vehicle damage
4. Insurance policy limits

All four impact the ultimate value of your case, so you should understand how and what each factor means.

FACTOR #1: LIABILITY

California is known as a "comparative fault" state. This means that state law requires a percentage of the blame is assigned to all involved parties for every motor vehicle accident. In some cases, fault will be black and white, and one party will be found 100% liable for the crash. However, other cases may mean multiple parties could have contributed to the accident.

As an example, let's say Bob and Karen, driving in separate cars and traveling in opposite directions, approach an intersection. Karen makes an unprotected left turn and hits Bob while he drives through.

If Bob followed all traffic laws when Karen hit him, Karen would be 100% at fault for the accident. However, on this occasion, Bob was speeding. Since both parties are partly to blame for the accident, a percentage of fault would be assigned to each. If Karen was assigned 80% and Bob 20%, Karen would be liable for 80% of Bob's damages, while Bob would be liable for 20% of Karen's.

HOW IS LIABILITY DETERMINED?

Fault percentage assigned to each person in the accident is apportioned based on the case's specific facts. The following is a summary of some of the general information that is considered when deciding fault after a car accident.

- Traffic code violations: You will likely be held at least partially liable if you violated the traffic code.

- Rear-end collisions: The accident is almost always your fault if you hit another driver from behind.

- Multi-vehicle rear-end collisions: If the car behind you hits you and pushes your vehicle into the car in front of you, the driver of the car that hit you will be at fault.

- Police reports: A police report stating that the other driver is at fault, violated a traffic code, or drove negligently, can greatly improve your case. Although the police report will not be admissible at trial, insurance adjusters find police officer opinions very convincing. Additionally, the police report will be admissible if your case goes to arbitration.

- Witnesses: Any third-party witnesses to the accident could corroborate your side of the story and sometimes even provide additional evidence in your favor. An impartial and trustworthy witness's statements and testimony will be given a lot of weight.

- Physical evidence: In some cases, physical evidence can be a determining factor when deciding liability. Physical evidence in your case may include vehicle position and damage after the crash, broken glass, skid marks, or debris.

FACTOR #2: INJURY SEVERITY AND TYPE

Injury severity and type significantly impact the value of your case, as more serious injuries almost always result in more damages. Your settlement amount can vary depending on a variety of factors, including:

- How much pain the injury caused
- Any permanent effects from the injury
- How serious and disfiguring these permanent effects are

- The amount of medical evidence available
- Medical treatment intensity and duration
- Recovery period length
- Medical bill costs
- Any wage loss suffered and the amount
- How much the injury affects daily life

An insurance adjuster considers all these factors when determining a settlement offer, as well as calculating all medical expenses related to the injury.

Insurance companies heavily rely on medical expenses in determining pain and suffering damages, which are typically proportional to each other. This means that two otherwise identical injuries could result in two vastly different settlements based on medical costs (i.e. more treatments).

Let's look at a few examples to put all this into context.

EXAMPLE #1

Carly and Jim are both in car crashes and suffer whiplash as a result. Carly only receives physical therapy treatment, while Jim receives physical therapy, sees his primary care physician several times, and has an x-ray and MRI scan. Jim will receive a higher settlement than Carly because he has more medical bills, and his pain and suffering damages will also likely increase.

EXAMPLE #2

Brian and Valerie are both in car accidents and receive similar injuries. They are both unable to attend work for three weeks due to their recovery. Brian's salary is $72,000 per year, whereas

Valerie's is $250,000. Since Valerie earns more than Brian, she will receive more money for lost wages than him.

EXAMPLE #3

Melanie and George both get into car crashes. They each suffer severe breaks in three fingers, causing a loss of fine motor skills. Melanie is an accountant, whereas George is a first chair violinist in an orchestra. George will receive compensation for his lost earning potential, causing his settlement to be larger than Melanie's, as she can still perform her job.

FACTOR #3: VEHICLE DAMAGE

Damage to vehicles is another significant factor in calculating your claim's value. Typically, the greater the damage to the cars, the greater the probability that the crash victims were severely injured.

For example, in cases where a similar injury was sustained, a claim involving $10,000 in property damage often receives a higher settlement than an accident resulting in $800 worth of damages.

You could struggle to get a settlement to cover your medical bills if the accident only caused some scratches to your vehicle.

FACTOR #4: INSURANCE POLICY LIMITS

Insurance policies have limits on the amount of money they will pay for a claim. This limit varies based on policy terms. In most cases, you can only recover damages up to the other driver's policy limit.

For example, if your case involves $20,000 of damages but the at-fault driver's policy limit is $15,000 per person, you can only recover $15,000.

Your insurance company is responsible for covering the difference if your damages exceed the policy limit and you have Underinsured Motorist (UIM) coverage — a policy for when the at-fault driver does not have sufficient coverage to pay your damages.

Likewise, you may not be able to receive any settlement at all if you are in an accident caused by an uninsured driver unless you have an Uninsured Motorist (UM) policy. If you do have UM coverage, your insurance company will pay for your damages.

If you are still confused about UIM and UM policies, don't worry — since this is such an important topic, I will go into more detail about UIM and UM coverage in chapter 7.

CAN I COLLECT THE REMAINING DAMAGES BY SUING THE OTHER DRIVER?

Yes, you can; however, it may not be a good idea to do so.

Litigation is expensive and time consuming. Even if the judge or a jury rules that the at-fault driver should pay you, for example, $5,000, it is often challenging to collect that amount from the defendant. Most people with low insurance coverage are "judgment-proof," which means they either don't have assets or have a very low-paying job. Even if the defendant pays the amount, you may end up with less because you could spend more on litigation.

So, personally suing the driver generally makes sense when the damages are high (i.e., you underwent surgery and incurred high medical expenses), you don't have insurance coverage for uninsured or underinsured drivers, and there's proof that the defendant has the means to pay.

IN SUMMARY

FACTOR #1: LIABILITY

Since California is a comparative fault state, each party is assigned a liability percentage for the car accident, based on the following factors:

- Traffic code violations
- Rear-end collisions
- Multi-vehicle rear-end collisions
- Police reports
- Witnesses
- Physical evidence

FACTOR #2: INJURY SEVERITY AND TYPE

Considerations that are weighed when deciding damages include:

- How much pain the injury caused
- Any permanent effects from the injury
- How serious and disfiguring these permanent effects are
- The amount of medical evidence available
- Medical treatment intensity and duration
- Recovery period length

- Medical bill costs
- Any wage loss suffered and the amount
- How much the injury affects daily life

FACTOR #3: VEHICLE DAMAGE

Typically, the greater the damage to the cars involved, the greater the probability that the crash victims were severely injured.

FACTOR #4: INSURANCE POLICY LIMITS

Damages are typically capped at the at-fault party's insurance policy limit. However, Underinsured Motorist (UIM) or Uninsured Motorist (UM) policies could cover your damages in certain situations.

GOT INTO
A BIG ACCIDENT
BROKE HIS ARM

SETTLEMENT $200,000

GOT INTO
A MINOR ACCIDENT
JUST SOME NECK PAIN

SETTLEMENT $7,000

GENERALLY,
THE MORE DAMAGE TO THE VEHICLE,
THE MORE SERIOUS THE INJURY,
THE HIGHER THE SETTLEMENT

Chapter 6
───

Do You Really Need a Lawyer?

A t this point, you may be wondering if you have to hire a lawyer to be paid for your injuries. The answer to this question is "no" — there's no requirement that you hire an attorney to receive compensation for your damages. You can simply negotiate a settlement without a lawyer and close the case.

The real question is, *should* you hire a lawyer?

It depends.

WILL HIRING A LAWYER GET YOU A BETTER SETTLEMENT?

While lawyers can help you receive a better settlement offer in most situations, you may not need an attorney to handle all claim types. In certain uncomplicated, minor-injury claims, an attorney will cost you more than they can increase your settlement — a good attorney will tell you this.

HOW DO ATTORNEY FEES WORK?

You should have a basic understanding of how attorney fees work when deciding to hire a lawyer.

First, way fees are assessed, which vary based on the type of attorney you need:

- Divorce lawyers usually bill by the hour
- Immigration attorneys typically charge a flat fee
- Personal injury lawyers generally work on a contingency basis

With contingency fees, you don't pay your lawyer anything upfront. Instead, you agree to give your attorney a fixed percentage of the settlement once the money is received. It's standard for personal injury lawyers to charge 33% to 45% of the compensation you receive in contingency fees.

For example, if the settlement is $10,000, and you agreed to pay your attorney one third, the contingency fees will then be $3,333.33. On the other hand, you don't owe anything to the attorney if you don't receive a settlement. A third of $0 is $0.

Statistically, people who hire attorneys receive higher settlements. Even after deducting attorney fees, they usually still walk away with more money than they would have received without an attorney.

WHY DO PEOPLE WITH LAWYERS GET MORE MONEY?

While this may be the first or second accident you've experienced in your life, personal injury lawyers handle them every day. Through experience, personal injury attorneys develop:

- Extensive knowledge of the law and insurance company tactics
- Strategies for dealing with insurance companies
- Understanding of the personal injury process
- Strong negotiation skills

On top of their skills and experience, personal injury lawyers offer various other benefits.

1. **Lawyers use investigators to help gather evidence that strengthens your claim**

   When your case involves assets, insurance, or liability, personal injury attorneys know what proof they need and how to get it.

2. **Level the playing field.**

   The other side will put their best foot forward, so you'll be dealing with their insurance representatives or lawyers. These experts are trained to negotiate aggressively, and you'll probably be in over your head if you tried to handle things yourself.

3. **An attorney can carry out the necessary complicated calculations to determine your damages in high-value claims**

   The severity of your injuries mostly determines the amount of compensation you receive for your accident. Generally, your medical expenses, lost income, and how long you remain in pain or disabled define your injuries' seriousness.

   As your medical bills and lost income increase, so does your compensation. However, the higher the number, the more difficult it is to gauge reasonable reimbursement and how much an insurance company is willing to shell out. Through knowledge and experience, a personal injury lawyer can navigate these complicated claims.

SOMETIMES, YOU ARE BETTER OFF WITHOUT A LAWYER

If your injuries and vehicle damages are minor, then you may be better off without a lawyer. For example, if your claim is simple, then an attorney can't do much to add to its value as the necessary paperwork and negotiation are insignificant and straightforward. In this case, a reputable personal injury lawyer should advise that you are likely to end up with more money if you handle the claim yourself.

Let's look at a hypothetical situation. Suppose you were in an accident and suffered minor neck pain. You received acupuncture treatments that cost $2,000. If you represented yourself and negotiated well, you could get yourself a $4,000 settlement, so you would receive $2,000 after paying off your medical bills.

If you hired a lawyer in this situation, then they may secure a slightly better settlement of $5,000. You would pay $1,666.67 in attorney fees (one third). After the $2,000 acupuncture bill and the attorney fee of $1,666.67, your net settlement is $1,333.33. As you can see, you would receive a higher total payment but a lower net settlement if you hired a lawyer in this instance.

Cases such as this also hurt law firms because certain costs are incurred with every case they take. The highest expenses are usually time spent and administration. Law firms are for-profit businesses, and if the fee they get is only $1,666.67, then this case will most likely be a loss for them.

Our firm occasionally takes a case that we know will not bring a profit. We do this to help the client when they are unlikely to receive compensation without legal representation. Unfortunately, we can't do this often because our resources are limited.

ONLINE COURSE TO NEGOTIATE CLAIMS WITHOUT A LAWYER

If you decide to handle the claim yourself or you can't find an attorney to take your case, I recommend the online course, "Winning Settlement Strategies," from Injury Claims 101 (www.injuryclaims101.com). The course teaches you about the personal injury claims process and how to negotiate the best possible settlement.

I have worked with several insurance claim adjusters to provide the content for this course, which consists of the following:

Module 1: All About Treatment & Bills: Legitimizing Your Claim

Module 2: Avoid Mistakes that Could Ruin Your Case: How to Open a Claim and Talk to an Adjuster

Module 3: Know What Your Case Is Worth: How to Calculate Your Settlement

Module 4: Understand the Mindset of the Insurance Adjuster to Maximize Your Settlement

Module 5: Gather Evidence to Prove Your Claim

Module 6: The Plug and Play Demand Letter

Module 7: How to Negotiate Your Settlement Like a Pro

The course includes 20 tools to help you implement what you're learning, so you can apply that knowledge to your injury claim. It also includes the following four bonuses:

1. Winning Settlement Strategies Workbook
2. Advanced Negotiation Tactics Guide
3. Five Types of Insurance Coverage You Should Know
4. Five Common Arguments Insurance Adjusters Make and How to Counter Them

OTHER REASONS TO HIRE A LAWYER

There are a few additional reasons why hiring a personal injury attorney can be a good idea when your injuries are serious:

1. Avoid the stress of dealing with insurance companies
Obtaining a settlement for your injuries after a car crash can be stressful. Hiring a personal injury lawyer can provide you with peace of mind, so you can concentrate on healing.

2. Get the medical attention you need
Medical expenses can be a considerable obstacle to your recovery if you don't have health insurance or Medpay. Personal injury lawyers can connect you with medical providers to treat you on what is called a "lien-basis." This means you won't have to pay until you get a settlement.

Your attorney's connections are meaningful because many healthcare providers will not offer medical treatment to patients under a lien. This is mainly because personal injury claims are not always successful in securing compensation.

Like all businesses offering services on credit, medical providers want to ensure you will pay them back. For this reason, the majority who work on a lien basis only accept patients with "winnable cases." A referral from an attorney whom the healthcare provider trusts can get you through the door.

Our firm works with various healthcare professionals willing to treat our clients on a medical lien. These include:

- Chiropractors
- Physical therapists
- Acupuncturists
- Family medicine
- Pain management
- Orthopedic specialists
- Neurologists
- Surgeons

Getting an appointment with a doctor can take weeks, even if you do have health insurance. Your attorney can immediately connect you to a lien-based medical provider if you need to start treatment sooner.

3. Represent you in litigation
Your case may need to go to court if the responsible party disputes your compensation claim. Even with legitimate personal injury claims, you can find yourself at a severe

disadvantage if the other party is represented by a lawyer and you aren't.

A personal injury attorney on your side levels the playing field because they gather all the evidence you need to win your case in court and receive maximum compensation.

4. Navigate complex cases

You should seek counsel from a personal injury lawyer as soon as possible if it is unclear who is at fault. In these types of situations, the other party's insurance company will almost always blame you for damages. You need an attorney in your corner to argue your case.

Similarly, if you were involved in an accident that included multiple parties, hiring a personal injury attorney will give you the best chance at success. Attorneys have the experience and skills necessary to deal with numerous insurance companies at once while building a case that protects their clients. When multiple people are at fault for your injury, a lawyer will also ensure you get the compensation you deserve for your injuries.

Finally, you should hire a lawyer if the insurance company denies or delays your claim. Insurance companies know that most people don't understand the complex laws and procedures involved and often use this advantage to deny legitimate injury claims because they think you can't do anything about it. They may also delay claims to slowly beat you into submission.

You should consult with a personal injury attorney as soon as possible in either of these situations.

WHAT SHOULD YOU LOOK FOR WHEN HIRING A LAWYER?

Find an attorney who practices personal injury cases exclusively. Personal injury law is complicated and involves many specialized rules and processes, so avoid general practice attorneys.

Choose an attorney who will go to trials, arbitrations, or mediations. Most personal injury lawyers are reluctant to take their cases to court, so they may pressure you to accept less than you deserve.

Attorneys with good, authentic reviews that talk about both the settlement itself and the firm's quality of service are excellent indicators.

Search for a firm that firmly believes in keeping clients up to date. The most common complaints against law firms include a lack of communication. Many of our clients left their previous attorney because they never received updates and their cases were significantly delayed.

A quality personal injury lawyer should also collaborate with you through each stage of your case. Securing compensation for your injury requires cooperation with your attorney, so make sure you feel comfortable with them.

IN SUMMARY

BENEFITS OF HIRING A LAWYER:

- You generally receive a better settlement
- Access to investigators that help gather evidence to strengthen your claim

- They are better equipped to negotiate a settlement
- They carry out the complicated calculations necessary to determine your damages in high-value claims
- To avoid the stress of dealing with insurance companies
- To help you get the medical attention you need
- Offers successful representation in litigation
- Can help you navigate complex cases

WHEN YOU ARE BETTER OFF WITHOUT A LAWYER:

- Your injuries are minor
- Vehicle damages are minor
- Your claim is simple, so an attorney can't do much to add to its value
- The necessary paperwork and negotiation are insignificant and straightforward

WHEN IT'S BETTER TO NOT HIRE A LAWYER

Chapter 7

Six Types of Car Insurance You Should Know About

It's essential you understand different insurance coverage types so that you're prepared if you are ever involved in an accident. In this chapter, we'll discuss the six types of car insurance policies you should know about.

1. LIABILITY COVERAGE

Liability coverage applies when you are the at-fault driver. This type of insurance covers both bodily injury and property damage.

- **Bodily injury** covers medical expenses for third parties injured in the accident. Your liability coverage will not reimburse you for any medical bills that you or your family members incur —medical payments insurance covers this.

- **Property damage** reimburses the cost to repair or replace physical property belonging to a third party, such as the vehicle or personal possessions damaged or destroyed in the crash.

MINIMUM LIABILITY COVERAGE IN CALIFORNIA

State law requires drivers to maintain minimum insurance on vehicles registered in California. Many auto insurance companies abbreviate the minimum coverage needed as **15/30/5**.

This means that your liability coverage provides up to:

- $15k ("15") in injury compensation to anyone injured in the accident
- $30k ("30) in total injury compensation to all injured parties
- $5k ("5") in reimbursement for damage to other people's property

It's important to remember that your liability coverage only reimburses third parties for their injuries and property damage. Additional coverage is needed if you want insurance for your own damages when you are at fault.

2. COLLISION COVERAGE

Collision coverage reimburses you when an object causes physical damage to your vehicle, for example:

- Another vehicle
- A pedestrian or bicyclist
- Other objects, such as trees, gates, buildings, guardrails, animals, or dumpsters

This type of coverage may have a **deductible** — the amount of money you'll have to pay out-of-pocket before your insurer reimburses any expenses.

Unlike liability coverage, which only covers damages to other vehicles when you are at fault, collision coverage means that you can repair your car regardless of the at-fault party.

When the other driver is at fault, their liability insurance will typically cover damages to your vehicle; however, you can file a claim against your own collision insurance if they do not have liability coverage.

3. UNINSURED AND UNDERINSURED MOTORIST COVERAGE

Uninsured Motorist (UM) coverage protects you if you are hit by a driver who does not have liability insurance or if you are involved in a hit-and-run crash. **Underinsured Motorist (UIM)** coverage applies if the at-fault driver has liability insurance but the limits are too low to pay for all your expenses.

UM/UIM coverage compensates you and your passengers for any damages the at-fault driver's insurance would have paid for if they'd had adequate coverage. Damages could include medical expenses, pain and suffering, lost income, and funeral costs.

You can purchase UM/UIM coverage through your own insurer. Contact your auto insurance provider if you're unsure if you have this coverage. Note that uninsured motorist coverage also covers underinsured drivers in California — no separate policy is required.

4. UNINSURED MOTORIST PROPERTY DAMAGE COVERAGE

Uninsured Motorist Property Damage (UMPD) coverage reimburses you for physical damage to your vehicle or other property in an accident caused by:

- A driver without liability insurance
- A driver who does not have enough liability insurance to cover all your damages
- A hit-and-run driver

California law allows you to add $3,500 of UMPD coverage to your policy if you don't have collision coverage.

5. MEDICAL PAYMENT COVERAGE

Medical Payment (MedPay) coverage reimburses medical expenses for you and your passengers, no matter who is at fault. MedPay is optional in California, so you can decide whether or not to add it to your policy.

MedPay could apply if you or your passenger are injured in a private motor vehicle, rideshare, or taxi accident. If you're injured, MedPay covers all reasonable and necessary medical expenses and funeral costs (up to the policy limit). Examples of reimbursable expenses include:

- Physician, dentist, and hospital bills
- Ambulance and EMT costs
- Treatment such as chiropractic adjustments, acupuncture, and physical or occupational therapy
- Diagnostic tests such as x-rays and MRIs

- Short and long-term care
- Medical supplies and prosthetics

6. COMPREHENSIVE COVERAGE

Comprehensive coverage pays when something other than a collision damages your vehicle. Many people confuse collision and comprehensive coverage because they both reimburse you for property damage; however, collision coverage only pays expenses related to a crash with another vehicle or object.

On the other hand, comprehensive coverage includes damage caused by:

- Theft
- Fire
- Vandalism
- Severe weather and natural disasters
- Falling objects, such as trees or branches
- Other events you didn't cause

Note that comprehensive insurance does not pay for regular maintenance or mechanical issues.

Bonus: A personal injury attorney's recommendation for your auto insurance policy

From my experience as a personal injury attorney specializing in car accidents, I have compiled some recommendations for the coverage your insurance policy should include.

1. Your assets are vulnerable when you're personally sued, and insufficient liability coverage can leave you at risk if the damage you cause exceeds your limits. Carry high liability coverage (at least $100K/$300K/$100K) if you have assets to protect or a young driver is on your policy.

2. Purchase collision coverage if you drive an expensive car or currently lease or finance a vehicle. For example, a client's luxury vehicle was totaled by a hit-and-run driver only a month after purchasing. My client now owes over $40,000 to the financing company. If they had collision coverage, they would have been able to recover the car's market value.

3. If you choose not to purchase collision coverage, at least consider uninsured motorist property damage (UMPD), which covers up to $3,500 in property damage.

4. I strongly advise drivers to purchase UM/UIM coverage. Approximately 20% of my clients were hit by drivers without insurance. If they didn't have this coverage, they would have had to cover damages for their injuries themselves — even if the collision wasn't their fault. At least two to three times a month, we receive calls from people seriously injured by a hit-and-run or uninsured driver, but we can't help them because they don't have UM/UIM coverage.

5. Get MedPay if your health insurance has high deductibles or if you don't have any insurance at all. With MedPay, you can start treatment (take an ambulance, get emergency care, etc.) without worrying if the at-fault driver's insurance will pay your bills. High-deductible health insurance means that you could be responsible for thousands of dollars in health

care costs before your insurance starts. The premium to add MedPay is usually minimal, often less than $5 a month.

It is vital for any driver to familiarize themselves with their auto insurance coverage. Carefully read your policy document, and contact your insurance company agent, or broker if you do not fully understand something in the policy.

IN SUMMARY

The six types of car insurance are:

1. **Liability coverage** pays for bodily injury and property damage caused to third parties when you are the at-fault driver.

2. **Collision coverage** reimburses you when an object physically damages your vehicle.

3. **Uninsured and Underinsured Motorist (UM/ UIM) coverage** compensate you if an uninsured, underinsured, or hit-and-run driver injures you.

4. **Uninsured Motorist Property Damage (UMPD) coverage** reimburses you for property damage caused by uninsured, underinsured, or hit-and-run drivers.

5. **Medical Payment (MedPay) coverage** will reimburse medical expenses for you and your passengers, no matter who is at fault.

6. **Comprehensive coverage** pays when something other than a collision damages your vehicle.

Chapter 8

Types of Insurance Adjusters

DEFINITION OF "ADJUSTER"

The insurance provider typically employs an "adjuster" or "claims adjuster" and assigns them to manage your claim. Adjusters review personal injury and property damage claims and decide how much they think the insurance company should pay.

1. PROPERTY DAMAGE ADJUSTER

Property damage adjusters handle vehicle repair, rental, and out-of-pocket reimbursement issues, such as towing fees and car seat replacement.

Property damage adjuster's duties include:

- Inspecting damages to the vehicle and personal property
- Preparing estimates

- Reviewing claimant-prepared estimates
- Negotiating settlement amounts with claimants
- Assisting with rental car coordination

2. TOTAL LOSS ADJUSTER

In situations where the vehicle is determined a total loss, the appropriate adjuster may be assigned to the claim to assist with the wrecked vehicle's valuation and any payment owed to the claimant. Sometimes, property damage adjusters also handle total losses.

A total loss adjuster is responsible for:

- Handling vehicle valuations
- Reviewing claimant-presenting appraisals
- Negotiating settlement amounts with claimants
- Working with salvage facilities
- Documenting salvage issues according to state statute

3. BODILY INJURY ADJUSTER

Bodily injury adjusters, sometimes called liability or main adjusters, handle the claim's personal injury portion. They gather the required information to valuate the injury claim, talk to the claimant or their attorney, and negotiate a settlement for bodily injury damages.

Bodily injury adjuster's duties entail:

- Evaluating and investigating the insurance policy's coverage and who is liable for the accident

- Obtaining records and documents from victims, the other driver, and physicians and taking recorded statements
- Communicating and negotiating settlements with victims and lawyers
- Interpreting medical records, reviewing medical bills, valuating the claim, and managing the claim's resolution process
- Determining the claim's value, issuing checks, and declining payments

4. MEDPAY ADJUSTER

MedPay adjusters work for the claimant's insurance company and approve or deny medical payment claims. MedPay covers medical costs for the victim and any passengers injured during a car accident.

MedPay adjusters are responsible for:

- Processing MedPay claim payments
- Advising injured parties of their policy benefits, limits, and exclusions
- Reviewing medical records and bills to determine proper settlements and checking for excessive treatment

While this is the typical setup, some variations exist between insurance providers — for example, certain claims are handled on a "team level," where no specific adjusters are assigned. A single adjuster may take the entire claim, including both property damage and bodily injury, but this is rare.

IN SUMMARY

The key players in a personal injury case:

- **Property damage adjusters** handle vehicle repair, rental, and out-of-pocket reimbursement issues.
- **Total loss adjusters** assist claimants with total loss settlements.
- **Bodily injury adjusters** handle the personal injury portion of the claim.
- **MedPay adjusters** work for the claimant's insurance company and approve or deny medical payment claims.

PART B

PROPERTY DAMAGE CLAIM

Chapter 9

Who Pays to Repair Your Car?

Examples of compensation you can receive for property damage to your vehicle include:

- Repair costs
- Rental car costs while your vehicle is being repaired
- "Loss of use" for the time your vehicle is being repaired if you didn't get a rental car
- Your vehicle's value depreciation caused by the repair
- Towing or transportation costs
- Your vehicle's fair market value if it's a total loss

You can also file a claim for any personal possessions damaged or destroyed, such as cell phones or laptops.

Let's take a look at an example.

Paul was involved in a car accident, and his vehicle was in the shop for ten days. The repair costs were $5,000 and the towing bill was $250. He rented a vehicle for $25 per day for ten days so that he could get to work while his car was being repaired.

Paul's cell phone was also damaged in the collision. He purchased it a few years ago for $800. He spent $50 for a repair estimate, only to find that it was beyond fixing. He found a few used cell phones (of the same model and age) for sale between $300 and $400.

The total property damage Paul could be compensated for is:

Auto towing	$250
Auto repair	$5,000
Rental car	$250
Cell phone repair estimate	$50
Cell phone value	$350
Total	$5,900

YOU HAVE A LEGAL DUTY TO MITIGATE YOUR DAMAGES, SO GET YOUR VEHICLE OUT OF STORAGE ASAP!

You are legally required to mitigate your duties by getting your vehicle out of storage — even if the accident wasn't your fault. This means that if your car was left inoperable and towed to a storage facility, you need to have it moved as soon as possible to reduce storage costs. The other driver's insurance company could refuse to pay your total costs if you let your car sit on a tow lot collecting fees.

Your insurance provider will pay for towing and storage if you have collision coverage; however, you need to contact them immediately after the accident to avoid processing delays.

You or your lawyer should immediately let the insurance company know if you can't move the vehicle from the tow yard due to financial or physical limitations. This will allow the insurance provider to quickly remove the vehicle.

USING YOUR INSURANCE COVERAGE VS. THE OTHER DRIVER'S INSURANCE COVERAGE

You can receive reimbursement for your property damage by filing a claim with either:

- The at-fault driver's liability insurance policy
- Your own collision insurance policy

You have only one option if you don't have collision coverage: the at-fault driver's insurance.

USING YOUR INSURANCE COLLISION COVERAGE TO FIX YOUR CAR

Not every insurance policy includes collision coverage, so you can only file a property damage claim with your insurer if you elected to add it to your policy.

A few advantages to using this method are:

1. IT'S FASTER THAN GOING THROUGH THE OTHER DRIVER'S LIABILITY INSURANCE BECAUSE COLLISION COVERAGE DOESN'T REQUIRE A FAULT DETERMINATION.

Investigations into determining the at-fault party can take days or even weeks, so collision coverage can get you back on the road much faster. For example, the other insurance company may argue that you were partially at fault or that their insured driver was not responsible for the crash at all. You may have to wait for the police report or obtain witness testimonies to prove the other driver was responsible. The insurance company could even delay the process, hoping you give in.

2. IF YOU'RE PARTIALLY AT FAULT FOR THE ACCIDENT, COLLISION STILL COVERS 100% OF YOUR DAMAGES (MINUS DEDUCTIBLES).

Use your collision coverage if you're partially at fault for the accident. Your owed compensation from the other driver's liability policy or your own insurance company in an uninsured motorist claim depends on the degree of responsibility the other driver had for the accident. Your compensation through the other driver's liability or your insurance's uninsured motorist coverage will reduce in proportion to your level of fault in the accident. This is called "comparative negligence."

However, fault is irrelevant if you file a property damage claim with your collision coverage.

3. YOU CAN AVOID TALKING TO THE AT-FAULT DRIVER'S INSURANCE COMPANY UNTIL THE FACTS OF THE ACCIDENT, INCLUDING THE EXTENT OF YOUR INJURIES, ARE CLEAR.

It is risky to discuss your accident with claims adjusters before you are 100% clear on the facts and your arguments. If you file a claim against your own collision policy, your insurer must reimburse you as soon as you comply with its inspection and estimates rules and agree to a repair amount.

WATCH OUT FOR DEDUCTIBLES!

Your reimbursement from your collision policy will reduce depending on your deductible amount. This is what you are required to pay out-of-pocket before your insurance kicks in, as specified by your policy. A large deductible can stand in the way of getting your car fixed if you need insurance money to pay for repairs.

For example, most people have a deductible between $500 to $1,000 on their collision policies. If your vehicle costs $5,000 to repair and you have a $1,000 deductible, your insurance will only reimburse you for $4,000, and you will have to pay the remainder. However, if the accident is not your fault, then the at-fault driver's insurance company will reimburse you for the amount of the deductible.

DO MY RATES GO UP IF I FILE A CLAIM WITH MY INSURANCE COMPANY WHEN I'M NOT AT FAULT?

Nope! Filing a claim with your insurance should not impact your rates; however, that you were in an accident might, even if you don't use a collision coverage.

USING THE AT-FAULT DRIVER'S INSURANCE LIABILITY COVERAGE TO FIX YOUR CAR

When another driver is at fault for your accident, you can file a property damage claim against their liability coverage to repair your vehicle. As previously discussed, the advantage of filing against the other driver's insurance is that there are no deductibles. However, the disadvantage is that you will have to wait for reimbursement if liability is unclear or contested, and this takes time to investigate.

For example, claim adjusters sometimes dispute how much their insured driver was at fault for the accident, or they may claim that they weren't responsible at all! You will have to wait until these disputes are settled before reaching an agreement about how much the liability insurer owes you. You can still file a collision claim with your own insurer (as long as you have coverage!) if settlement is taking too long.

Note that in certain situations, the other driver's liability insurer may suggest that you use your collision coverage to repair your vehicle due to a limit issue. A low at-fault driver's policy limit may not cover the full cost of fixing your vehicle. If this is the case, you should repair your vehicle using your collision coverage and request reimbursement for the deductible.

WHAT IF YOU DON'T HAVE COLLISION COVERAGE AND THE OTHER DRIVER IS UNINSURED?

Uninsured Motorist Property Damage (UMPD) cover works the same as collision coverage (up to your limit). If you don't have UMPD, then you will have to pay out of your own pocket.

Of course, there's always the option to file a personal injury lawsuit against the at-fault driver in court.

IN SUMMARY

For **property damage** (such as repairs to your vehicle), you can file a claim against either:

- The at-fault driver's liability insurance policy
- Your own collision insurance policy

COMPENSABLE PROPERTY DAMAGE EXAMPLES:

- Repair costs
- Rental car costs while your vehicle is being repaired
- "Loss of use" for the time your vehicle is being repaired if you didn't get a rental car
- Your vehicle's depreciation value caused by the repair
- Towing or transportation costs
- Your vehicle's fair market value if it's a total loss

COLLISION COVERAGE:

- Is faster than going through the other driver's liability insurance because it doesn't require a fault determination
- Still pays 100% of your damages if you're partially at fault
- Means you can avoid talking to the at-fault driver's insurance until the facts of the accident, including the extent of your injuries, are clear
- Requires you to pay a deductible

AT-FAULT DRIVER'S LIABILITY COVERAGE:

- No deductible
- You will have to wait until fault is determined
- There may be a limit issue

YOU SHOULD USE COLLISION COVERAGE WHEN:

- The other driver's insurer delays the liability decision and you need to fix your car ASAP
- You are partially at fault
- The other driver's property damage liability limit is too low

You should use the other driver's liability coverage when your collision deductible is too high.

Chapter 10

General Process of Getting Your Car Repaired

STEP #1: CONTACT THE INSURANCE COMPANY AND ARRANGE FOR A PROPERTY DAMAGE ADJUSTER TO INSPECT DAMAGES TO YOUR VEHICLE

As discussed in chapter 8, sometimes two different insurance adjusters handle personal injury and property damage in car crash claims:

- Property damage claims relate to vehicle repairs and any personal possessions damaged in the accident.
- Personal injury claims deal with physical injuries from the car crash. These claims are usually more complicated than property damage.

Whenever you speak to an insurance adjuster about property damage, don't say anything that could potentially diminish your personal injury claim (e.g., I'm feeling better, I'm doing well, etc.). Even if a different adjuster handles the personal injury claim, they both work for the same company and share information.

Since the property damage claim is usually handled first, you should limit your discussion to property damage (and only property damage). If you have an attorney, Do NOT discuss the accident itself, your injuries, medical treatment you are receiving, or any other information regarding your medical condition. If the adjuster asks, you should politely decline to comment and inform the adjuster to contact your attorney. If you are handling the case yourself without an attorney, you can provide a general description of your injuries, and state that you do not know the full extent of your injuries yet.

STEP #2: DAMAGE INSPECTION

The insurance provider covering the property damage claim has the right to inspect the damage to the vehicle to estimate the repair costs.

Damage inspection generally occurs in one of three ways:

1. The insurance company may inquire about your car's location, and a field adjuster will physically inspect the vehicle.

2. If the car is drivable, they may ask you to bring your vehicle to one of their body shops for inspection.

3. If you'd like to use a specific body shop, then the adjuster will work with them to obtain the inspection report and approve or deny the estimate.

DO YOUR RESEARCH

Before choosing a repair shop, make sure you carry out due diligence to ensure that the mechanic has proper qualifications and a good reputation and thoroughly identifies all damages. Reading online reviews or asking friends or family for personal recommendations is a great way to do this.

WHAT HAPPENS AFTER THE INSPECTION?

The body shop will inspect the damages and send their estimate to the adjuster for approval. The insurance company will sometimes send a field adjuster to the body shop to conduct an additional inspection. After a day or two, the property damage adjuster will typically send you or your body shop a copy of the repair estimate, and the body shop will begin the repair.

STEP #3: THE BODY SHOP BEGINS THE REPAIR

It's important to remember that you have the right to get the vehicle repaired at a body shop of your choice; there is no obligation to take the car to an in-network shop.

The mechanic may discover additional hidden damage during repair. If this occurs, the body shop will submit a supplement request to the insurance provider to receive additional repair cost. You will typically not be involved in this part of the process.

STEP #4: ONCE THE REPAIRS ARE COMPLETE, YOU CAN PICK UP YOUR CAR

If you think that problems still exist with the vehicle or that it was shoddily repaired, document the issues immediately. Take as many pictures and videos as possible, then return the car to the repair shop and ask them to fix the issues.

WHAT IF I DON'T WANT TO REPAIR MY CAR — CAN I JUST KEEP THE CHECK?

It is entirely up to you whether you want to repair your car. You will receive a check for the repair, so you choose to do with it as you see fit. While you can use the money to get your vehicle fixed, you can also just keep it.

IN SUMMARY

Step #1: Contact the insurance company and arrange for a property damage adjuster to inspect the damages to your vehicle.

Step #2: Property Damage adjuster inspects the vehicle. Damage inspection can occur in one of three ways:

1. A field adjuster physically inspects the vehicle at its location
2. You bring your vehicle to one of the insurance's body shops
3. The adjuster works with your chosen body shop

Step #3: The body shop repairs the vehicle. It's important to remember that you have the right to repair your vehicle at a body shop of your choice; you do not need to take your car to a specific place.

Step #4: Once the repairs are complete, pick up your car. If you think problems still exist or that work is shoddy once the repairs have been completed, immediately document the issues by take pictures and videos, then return the vehicle to the repair shop.

Step 1: Contacting the insurance company to report the accident

Property damage adjuster asking which body shop he would like to use, and arrange a date/time for the inspection

Step 2: Insurance adjuster inspecting the damaged vehicle

Step 3: Body shop repairing the vehicle

Step 4: Body shop calling the client that the repair is done

Chapter 11

Getting a Rental and Full Reimbursement for Out-of-Pocket Expenses

If you've been in a car crash, you are entitled to reimbursement for rental car costs or "loss of use" of your vehicle, as well as other out-of-pocket expenses.

RENTAL CAR AND LOSS OF USE

The at-fault driver's insurance policy should either provide you with a rental car for the time your vehicle is being repaired or pay you a reasonable rental price for a similar vehicle for the amount of time your car is out of commission.

USE YOUR OWN INSURANCE POLICY IF YOU HAVE RENTAL COVERAGE

I recommend you use rental car coverage if it's part of your insurance policy. It is much easier to use your own rental coverage, where your provider can set up "direct billing" with the rental company. This means you can pick up a car using a reservation code, and the insurance company are billed. You'll most likely have to provide a credit card, but your insurance company should cover everything as long as you rent a vehicle they approve and you return the car on time.

It's important to remember that your insurance policy terms may limit daily rental costs and length of renting the vehicle. For example, if your policy limit is $25 per day for 20 days, you'll have to start paying on the 21st day even if the repair of your vehicle is not done yet.

Also keep in mind that your insurance policy does not cover rental insurance or gas costs.

YOU CAN USE THE AT-FAULT DRIVER'S INSURANCE TO GET A RENTAL

The at-fault driver's insurance company will sometimes agree to set up direct billing with the rental car company, so you don't have to pay anything out of pocket. However, more often, they will require you to pay first and only reimburse the rental cost once you submit the receipt.

If you need a rental right away but the at-fault driver's insurance provider takes too long to accept the liability for the accident, then you may have to cover the cost of a rental yourself and seek reimbursement as part of the settlement.

HOW MANY DAYS AM I ENTITLED TO A RENTAL CAR?

You are entitled to rental car reimbursement for a reasonable amount of time it takes to repair the vehicle's damage.

If the car is not drivable after your accident, then you have the right to a rental from the accident date to the repair completion date. If the car was drivable after the accident, then you can get a rental from the date the repair started until the date the repair is completed.

WHAT KIND OF CAR CAN I RENT?

You're entitled to rent a vehicle that is reasonable and comparable to your own damaged car. This means that you can't rent a luxury car and expect reimbursement for $300 per day of rental costs when your car is a standard one. Similarly, don't get an SUV when your car is a sedan.

You should make a request to the property damage adjuster before you rent a car if you need a specific vehicle for work — for example, a work van. Just make sure you discuss this with the insuring company before incurring any out-of-pocket expenses.

LOSS OF USE DAMAGES

You are entitled to compensation for "loss of use" of your vehicle, if you don't rent a car while your car is being repaired. The amount of loss of use reimbursement you are entitled to in California is the cost of renting a similar vehicle for a reasonable amount of time while your vehicle needs repairs. If your car was totaled in the accident, you're entitled to loss of use damages for the amount of time reasonably necessary to replace the vehicle.

This means you can borrow someone else's car and receive a per diem payment, typically between $15 and $35 per day, for loss of use. For instance, if your vehicle's reasonable rental value is $30/day and the repair takes seven days, then you would be entitled to $210 ($30 x 7) in loss of use compensation.

Tip: If you have a spare car, or if you can borrow one from your friend or family, it could be better to just collect the loss of use damages.

WHAT IF I JUST DECIDED TO USE ALTERNATIVE TRANSPORTATION, SUCH AS UBER, LYFT, OR PUBLIC BUSES?

If you don't rent a car and you'd like to use alternative transportation, make sure you save receipts or other proof of payment to be reimbursed.

Note: "Double dipping" is not allowed. This means that if you receive a rental car, you won't be able to claim loss of use damages or out-of-pocket transportation expenses for the rental duration.

For instance, if you rent a car from the at-fault driver's insurance company for ten days but decide to take an Uber to work, you would not be able to receive reimbursement for the Uber cost. Similarly, you also can't receive loss of use damages for the ten days you have the rental.

DIMINISHED VALUE CLAIM

In addition to rental car or loss of use expenses, you are also entitled to reimbursement for your vehicle's "diminished value." Your car being in an accident can significantly decrease its value because many people expect a substantial discount when purchasing a car that has been in a crash.

Diminished value is calculated by subtracting the vehicle's reduced value after the repair from its market value before the crash. You'll need to hire an experienced appraiser to determine the amount.

A few essential things to keep in mind when dealing with diminished value:

- The sum of the cost of repairs and diminished value cannot exceed the car's market value before the crash.
- You cannot receive diminished value damages unless the leasing company charges you a damage fee.
- Diminished value can only be recovered from the at-fault driver's insurance, not your own.

DAMAGED PERSONAL PROPERTY

You are also entitled to recover the Actual Cash Value (ACV) of personal property damaged or destroyed in the accident, such as a car seat or laptop. The process of determining ACV for personal property is a little more complicated than for vehicles.

First, you must prove that the property you are claiming for was damaged at the time of the accident. You can usually do this by providing evidence, such as before-and-after photos of the object.

The next step is to show the property's market value by finding an item of a similar age and condition and the sell prices. The cost of replacing the property can also be informative when determining ACV if the object is reasonably new.

PROPERTY DAMAGE REIMBURSEMENT COSTS

Finally, you can be reimbursed for costs related to property damage, such as towing and storage fees. These expenses can be provided through receipts or other proof of payment. Make sure you don't forget to mitigate your damages and get your vehicle out of storage ASAP!

IN SUMMARY

RENTAL CAR AND LOSS OF USE

The at-fault driver's insurance policy should either provide you with a rental car for the time your vehicle is being repaired or pay you a reasonable rental price for a similar vehicle for the duration your car is out of commission.

TIPS:

- Use your own insurance policy if you have rental coverage.
- You can use the at-fault driver's insurance to get a rental.
- You are entitled to rental car reimbursement for the amount of time reasonably necessary to repair or replace the vehicle.
- You can rent a vehicle that is reasonable and comparable to your own damaged car.
- You are entitled to compensation for "loss of use," if you don't rent a vehicle.
- You can be reimbursed for out-of-pocket expenses if you don't rent a car and prefer to use alternative transportation.

DIMINISHED VALUE CLAIM

You are also entitled to reimbursement for your vehicle's "diminished value," which is calculated by subtracting the vehicle's reduced value after the repair from its market value before the crash.

DAMAGED PERSONAL PROPERTY

Actual Cash Value (ACV) of personal property damaged or destroyed in the accident, such as a car seat or laptop can also be recovered. You must prove that the property was damaged at the time of the accident. The next step is showing the property's market value by finding a similar item and its price.

PROPERTY DAMAGE REIMBURSEMENT COSTS

You can be reimbursed for costs related to property damage, such as towing and storage fees.

DOES NOT HAVE A CAR BECAUSE THE CAR IS AT THE BODY SHOP

TAKING UBER TO GET TO THE DOCTOR'S APPOINTMENTS

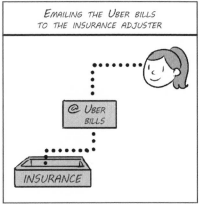

EMAILING THE UBER BILLS TO THE INSURANCE ADJUSTER

RECEIVES A CHECK FOR THE UBER BILLS

Chapter 12

Total Loss

Property damages will look a little different if your vehicle is a total loss. In this chapter, we'll discuss what you need to know about total loss auto insurance claims.

DEFINITION OF TOTAL LOSS

Your car is considered a "total loss" if it is so damaged from the accident that repair costs are greater than its Actual Cash Value (ACV). An insurance company only has to pay you the ACV of a totaled vehicle and not the cost to fix it.

Insurance providers in California use a "total loss formula" (TLF) to decide if your vehicle is totaled:

COST OF REPAIRS + SALVAGE VALUE* ≥ ACTUAL CASH VALUE

In other words, a car is a total loss when the cost to fix it plus the salvage value is greater than or equal to the ACV.

*The salvage value is equal to the price the wrecked vehicle could be sold at. In most cases, this amount will just be the cost of scrap metal; however, working components can be sold too.

EXAMPLES

Let's take a look at some examples to see how TLF plays out in real life.

SITUATION #1

Jennifer is t-boned at an intersection and her vehicle is seriously damaged. It would cost $12,000 to repair her car. Its salvage value is $500. Jennifer's car has an actual cash value of $10,000.

Jennifer's TLF would be:
$12,000 + $500 > $10,000

Since $12,500 is greater than $10,000, her vehicle would be a total loss, and the insurance company would pay her the ACV of $10,000.

SITUATION #2

Ryan's car is damaged in an accident. His vehicle needs $4,000 of repairs and has a salvage value of $3,000. The actual cash value is $16,000.

Ryan's TLF would be:
$4,000 + $3,000 < $16,000

Because $7,000 is less than $16,000, his car is not totaled, and the insurer would owe him the cost of the repairs ($4,000).

TOTAL LOSS INSURANCE PAYOUTS

You have the right to decide to keep or surrender your vehicle to the insurance company.

SURRENDERING

If you surrender the vehicle to the insurance company by transferring the title, you'll be paid the Actual Cash Value. It's essential to keep in mind that ACV is the car's fair market value (it's current sale price). ACV is not how much you paid for the vehicle or your auto loan's outstanding balance.

KEEPING

The insurance provider will pay you the ACV minus the salvage value if you want to keep the totaled vehicle. Essentially, you'll purchase the car back from the insurer for the salvage value. Keep in mind that you'll have to re-register the vehicle with the California Department of Motor Vehicles if you decide to keep it. A salvage certificate will also be on the title.

WHAT IF YOU DISAGREE WITH THE VALUATION?

You can challenge the insurance company's ACV calculation if you believe it is incorrect. The provider will typically request that you submit documentation supporting your argument. The insurance company may adjust its offer if you can submit credible evidence.

One source of evidence showing the vehicle's market value is Kelley Blue Book (www.kbb.com). You can also find comparable cars (year, make, model, and condition) for sale on cars.com or another similar website. However, an appraisal done by an expert will have more weight.

WHAT IF YOU WERE LEASING OR FINANCING?

The insurance provider will pay off the loan or lease directly before giving you the remaining payout.

However, it's possible that the ACV is less than your current outstanding balance. This typically happens with vehicles purchased new and financed for the full purchase price or luxury vehicles that lose a lot of market value from simply being driven off the lot. In these situations, you will be responsible for paying any remaining balance on the loan or lease.

For example, if you totaled a financed car with an actual cash value of $20,000 and the remaining amount on the loan is $30,000, you will have to pay the remaining $10,000 to the loan company, even if the accident was not your fault.

GAP INSURANCE

Some car dealers and auto lenders sell Guaranteed Auto Protection (GAP) insurance to help you avoid situations like the above. This coverage pays the difference between what you owe on your loan and your vehicle's ACV.

So, using the above example, you will not owe the financing company anything because GAP insurance would cover the $10,000.

RENTAL AND LOSS OF USE DAMAGES IF THE CAR IS A TOTAL LOSS

In the last chapter, we discussed reimbursement you can receive for renting costs while your car is being repaired. This also applies to a total loss situation; the only difference being the duration it covers.

If the car is being repaired, it's fairly simple: you're reimbursed for the time it takes until the car is repaired. However, it becomes more complicated if it was a total loss.

When your vehicle is totaled, you are entitled to receive rental reimbursement or loss of use damages for a reasonable amount of time it takes to replace your vehicle. While an insurance provider may argue that you can only receive loss of use damages until they make their first offer, you are entitled to receive damages until a few days after you receive your settlement check.

IN SUMMARY

DEFINITION OF TOTAL LOSS

Your car is considered a "total loss" if it is so damaged from the accident that repair costs are greater than its Actual Cash Value (ACV). An insurance company only has to pay you the ACV of a totaled vehicle and not the cost to fix it.

TOTAL LOSS FORMULA

Insurance providers in California use a "total loss formula" (TLF) to decide if your vehicle is totaled:

Cost of Repairs + Salvage Value ≥ Actual Cash Value

TOTAL LOSS INSURANCE PAYOUTS

You have the right to decide to keep or surrender your vehicle to the insurance company. You'll be paid the **Actual Cash Value** if you surrender the vehicle to the insurance company. On the other hand, the insurance provider will pay you the **ACV minus the salvage value** if you want to keep the totaled vehicle.

- You can challenge the insurance company's ACV calculation if you believe it is incorrect.
- The insurance provider pays off loans or leases directly before giving you the remaining portion.
- You are responsible for paying any remaining balance on a loan or lease If the ACV is less than your current outstanding balance.
- You can use Guaranteed Auto Protection (GAP) insurance coverage to pay the difference between the amount you owe on your loan and your vehicle's ACV.
- You are entitled to rental reimbursement or loss of use damages for the reasonable amount of time it takes to replace your vehicle.

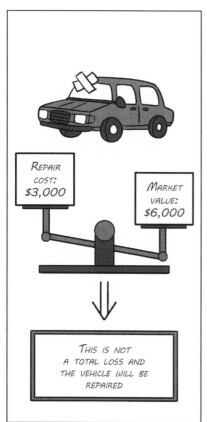

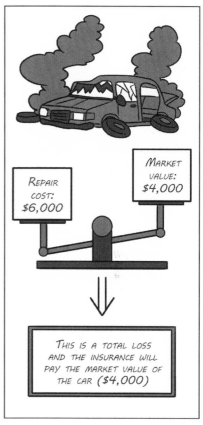

PART C

BODILY INJURY CLAIM

Chapter 13

Types of Car Accident Injuries

Injuries from car accidents can range from minor to severe. With so many different types, it's important to identify what kind of injuries you may have sustained so that you can receive the proper medical treatment and protect your right to fair compensation. In this chapter, we'll go over some common types of car accident injuries and how they affect your body.

SOFT TISSUE

Soft tissue injuries often occur in car accidents and are essentially trauma to a muscle, tendon, or ligament. The most common types of car crash soft tissue injuries include:

- Sprains
- Strains
- Lacerations (cuts)
- Abrasions (scrapes)
- Contusions (bruises)

However, because soft tissue injuries do not involve broken bones or damage to internal organs, insurance claim adjusters view these injuries as less severe than other types. Unfortunately, it can be challenging to prove soft tissue injuries because they usually cannot be verified with diagnostic tools such as an x-ray, unlike other traumatic injuries.

For this reason, it's essential you seek medical treatment as soon as possible after the accident — even if you aren't sure you've been injured. Medical records from immediately after the crash are the strongest evidence to have to prove the nature and extent of your soft tissue injuries (and that they were caused by the accident).

WHIPLASH

Whiplash is a type of soft tissue injury that occurs when your head snaps back and forth forcefully. This can happen as the result of a car crash impact and is particularly common for drivers and passengers in a vehicle that has been rear-ended. Although insurance companies usually view whiplash as a "minor" injury, it can cause pain and discomfort for weeks, months, or even years after the accident.

Whiplash symptoms vary from person to person, but your symptoms may include:

- Neck pain/stiffness that worsens with movement
- Reduced range of motion in the neck
- Headaches starting from the base of the skull
- Pain/tenderness in your shoulders, upper back, or arms

As with other injuries, it's important to seek immediate medical treatment for whiplash injuries to document your condition and avoid worsening or long-lasting symptoms.

BULGES AND HERNIATED DISCS

Car accidents can cause or worsen bulging and herniated discs, which are injuries to cartilage layers that serve as cushions between the bones in your spine (vertebrae). Discs are made of an exterior layer of tough cartilage surrounding softer cartilage in the middle.

BULGING DISCS

A bulging disc happens when movement causes the soft cartilage layer fluid to swell outward through the weakest point of the outer disc without breaking through. This creates a protrusion or bulge that can cause:

- Pain/tingling in your neck, fingers, hands, arms, or shoulders
- Pain in your feet, thighs, buttocks, or lower spine
- Difficulty walking
- Feeling weak when lifting or holding objects

HERNIATED DISCS

A herniated disc occurs when the soft interior cartilage pushes through a crack in the surrounding tough cartilage. While some herniated discs will not cause any symptoms, others might cause:

- Pain in your back, arms, legs, or feet
- Muscle spasms or weakness

- Numbness in your legs, hands, or feet
- A tingling or burning sensation
- A stiff neck

Disc injuries can lead to long-term, debilitating pain, so it's crucial to receive prompt diagnosis and treatment if you believe you have a bulging or herniated disc.

BROKEN BONES

Broken bones, also known as fractures, are a common type of car accident injury. They occur when a bone is completely or partially cracked or broken due to trauma or another type of impact. Fractures are classified as "open" when the bone breaks through the skin and "closed" when the skin remains intact.

While open fractures are generally immediately apparent, it can be challenging to tell if you have a closed fracture — particularly if the bone remains in its normal position.

Some signs that you may have broken a bone during a car crash include:

- Pain, swelling, bruising, tenderness, or deformity around the injured area
- Hearing or feeling a snap or grinding sound when the injury occurs
- Feeling pain when the injured area is touched, pressed, or moved

However, you may not feel much pain at all if the fracture is minor. This is another reason you should always seek treatment after a motor vehicle crash.

KNEE INJURIES

Your knee is one of the most important joints in your body, and it can be seriously injured when involved in a car accident. Injuries to your knee joint can affect your ability to walk, climb stairs, or kneel.

Car accident victims can suffer from several types of knee injuries, the most common of which are detailed below.

POSTERIOR CRUCIATE LIGAMENT (PCL) AND MEDIAL COLLATERAL LIGAMENT (MCL) INJURIES

PCL and MCL injuries are often referred to as "dashboard knee," as they are commonly caused by hitting your knee on the car's dashboard. However, they can be caused by the knee hitting any hard object in the car or being violently forced backward. These injuries affect the ligaments connecting your tibia (shinbone) to your femur (thighbone) and can cause pain and swelling in the injured area.

CARTILAGE TEARS

Similar to the spine, the knee contains cartilage discs that prevent friction between the bones and provide cushioning when you walk. Traumatic impacts such as a car crash can cause disc tears or other damage. Some of the most common symptoms caused by a cartilage tear are swelling, extreme pain, and locking.

FOOT AND ANKLE INJURIES

Feet and ankles are one of the most common areas for car accident injuries. Several types of foot and ankle injuries can occur, including sprains, fractures, and dislocations, all of which can reduce your mobility and cause severe pain.

Some common foot and ankle injuries include:
- Sprains and strains to the ligaments, tendons, and muscle tissues
- Fractures to ankle or foot bones
- Soft tissue injuries

Foot and ankle injuries can cause various symptoms, such as:

- Sudden, severe pain
- Swelling, bruising, and tenderness
- Inability to stand on the injured foot
- Stiffness
- Feeling warm to the touch
- Visible deformity

WRIST AND HAND INJURIES

Car crashes can also cause injuries to wrists and hands. This type of damage typically occurs when your hands come into contact with something hard during an accident, such as the steering wheel or dashboard.

Some of the most common wrist and hand injuries auto accident victims sustain include bruises, fractures, and damage to the ligaments, tendons, and muscles. A crash can also cause a finger to dislocate if it is forced into a bent position.

A few signs that you may have suffered a wrist or hand injury in a car crash include:

- Swelling, discoloration, or bruising
- Stiffness or numbness
- Pain or warmth in your hands, fingers, or wrists
- Difficulty moving or bending your fingers or wrists
- Diminished grip strength
- Burning or tingling in your wrists or hands

CONCUSSION

A concussion is a type of mild traumatic brain injury that can happen when an impact, such as a car accident, causes rapid head movement. Concussions may also occur after a blow to the head. Symptoms can include:

- Headaches
- Dizziness
- Nausea and vomiting
- Lack of coordination
- Sensitivity to light
- Confusion and memory loss
- Ringing in the ears
- Fatigue and tiredness

Concussions are not always easy to recognize because they can be temporary and sometimes resolve on their own in days or weeks. Signs and symptoms also vary between individuals depending on age and injury severity. Immediately seek medical treatment if you think you have sustained a concussion after being injured in a car accident.

TRAUMATIC BRAIN INJURY

People involved in car crashes are at risk of suffering traumatic brain injury (TBI) — an injury caused by the sudden impact of any outside force coming into contact with the head. In a motor vehicle accident, TBI commonly occurs when a victim hits their head on the steering wheel or an airbag, but it can also be caused by an object penetrating the skull.

A wide variety of TBI symptoms range in severity, from a mild concussion to a total loss of consciousness, long-term memory loss, coma, or even death. Some other symptoms might include:

- Amnesia, confusion, or other cognitive issues
- Difficulty speaking or slurred speech
- Difficulty concentrating, thinking, or understanding
- Inappropriate emotions
- Aggression, irritability, or impulsivity
- Dizziness or fainting
- Dilated or uneven pupils
- Nausea or vomiting
- Blurred vision
- Sensitivity to light

While it is common for car crash victims to experience headaches after the accident, what you think is a minor annoyance may actually be a symptom of an undiagnosed TBI. So, make sure a medical professional checks out any headaches you experience after a crash.

DAMAGE TO INTERNAL ORGANS

If you have been involved in a car crash, it is essential to know that your injuries may not always be visible. Injuries to internal organs can easily go undetected when you only look at the outside of the body because they do not show externally.

However, internal organ injuries can be life-threatening if left untreated. High-impact accidents in particular can cause damage to the organs, causing internal bleeding or the organ shutting down entirely. While any internal organ can be damaged in a car crash, livers and kidneys are typically the most injured.

Common symptoms of internal bleeding caused by organ damage include:

- Abdominal pain and swelling
- Lightheadedness, dizziness, or fainting from blood loss
- Loss of color in the face
- Fatigue
- Ecchymosis (a large area of purple skin)

Despite these symptoms, organ damage can be difficult to detect without a medical professional performing an x-ray or other imaging tests.

SPINAL CORD INJURIES

Car accidents are one of the leading causes of spinal cord injuries, which can range from mild to severe. However, the impact on the victim is often life-altering, as the damage to the spine can lead to loss of feeling, paralysis, or numbness in certain areas. Spinal cord injuries from car crashes are often caused by a sudden blow to the spinal cord or its surrounding tissues, such as ligaments, discs, and vertebrae.

LOSS OF LIMB AND AMPUTATION

Unfortunately, car crashes can result in drivers or passengers losing hands, feet, arms, legs, fingers, or toes after being cut by a sharp piece of metal or crushed in the accident. Sometimes, the force of the accident will sever the appendance on the scene. This is known as "traumatic amputation." In other situations, the limb or digit will be so severely damaged by the collision that surgical amputation is needed to prevent further injury or death.

FACIAL INJURIES

Facial injuries are one of the most common types of trauma victims suffer in motor vehicle crashes. These can be very painful and have long-term consequences for your appearance and quality of life. Facial injuries are often caused by flying debris, shattered glass, or contact with an airbag, but they can also occur when the occupant is ejected from the vehicle.

Car accident facial injuries may include:

- Soft tissue injuries
- Bone fractures
- Burns, cuts, and scrapes (and resulting scarring)
- Deformities
- Damage to the eyes

PTSD

Even the most minor car accident can cause victims to develop post-traumatic stress disorder, commonly known as PTSD. PTSD is a psychiatric disorder that impacts people who have experienced a traumatic event, such as a car crash.

PTSD victims may experience powerful and distressing thoughts and feelings about the traumatic experience for months or even years after the event. Symptoms of PTSD often include:

- Reliving the trauma in dreams or waking flashbacks
- Persistent fear, anger, or sadness
- Depression and anxiety
- Insomnia
- Loss of appetite
- Isolation from loved ones

Chapter 14

Treatment Types for Accident Victims

Throughout this book, I've stressed the importance of seeking treatment for your car crash injuries. However, many different types of treatment are available to car accident victims, and which treatment is right for you depends on the severity and nature of your injuries. In this chapter, we'll break down the various types of treatment you can pursue, so you can make informed healthcare decisions after a car crash.

EMERGENCY ROOM

The emergency room (ER) is your first choice to treat serious injuries you sustain in a car accident. As previously discussed, if you are injured from a major crash, you should accept an ambulance to the emergency room from the scene of the collision. However, there are some situations where a post-accident trip to urgent care is the better choice.

You should go to the ER for serious injuries, such as broken bones, severe burns, difficulty breathing, intense pain, or uncontrollable bleeding. For minor injuries, you can go to nearby urgent care. The most important thing is that you seek some sort of medical treatment after a car accident if you have any symptoms or injuries.

CHIROPRACTIC CARE

Chiropractors perform spinal manipulations, deep tissue massages, and trigger point therapy to ensure the body's musculoskeletal structure is correctly aligned. Chiropractic treatment is most commonly used on the spine and other joints to restore mobility after a traumatic event like a car crash. It can also be used as an alternative pain relief treatment for muscles, joints, bones, and connective tissues, and can be combined with conventional medical treatment. Below are the main benefits of chiropractic care:

- Reduces pain and inflammation
- Reduces scar tissue
- Restore range of motion

ACUPUNCTURE

Acupuncture is a treatment using thin needles that are inserted into the skin. It has been used for over 2,000 years to treat a variety of medical conditions and comes with various health benefits. In recent decades, acupuncture has grown in popularity in the United States as a complementary therapy for pain management.

Acupuncture can be used to:

- Reduce pain by increasing blood flow to injured areas
- Reduce headaches or migraines
- Reduce inflammation
- Improve organ functioning and immunity

PHYSICAL THERAPY

Physical therapy (also known as physiotherapy) is a type of healthcare that deals with the diagnosis and treatment of physical injuries and illnesses that limit movement. It's offered to patients who have been injured in car accidents to help them improve flexibility, increase strength, and reduce pain.

Two general types of physical therapy include hands-on treatment, where a physiotherapist touches your body when you are still, and movement-based treatment, where you're encouraged to move while being treated, such as walking or performing exercises. Treatment can include anything from personalized strengthening exercises to manual therapy, such as soft tissue mobilization (STM), stretching your muscles, using heat or cold packs on sore areas, or applying electric stimulation (TENS) for pain management.

GENERAL PHYSICIAN

General physicians, also known as family doctors or primary care physicians, are medically trained to prevent, diagnose, and treat a wide range of injuries and illnesses in the general population. Primary care physicians usually build long-term relationships with their patients and provide them with comprehensive healthcare.

If you have been injured in a car accident, then your general physician may be able to evaluate minor injuries and provide necessary treatment. They can also help you with ongoing pain management and other continuing concerns. If the injuries are severe, they will refer you to a specialist.

PAIN MANAGEMENT SPECIALIST

Pain management specialists are medical professionals who specialize in treating chronic and acute pain conditions for people with injuries, including those caused by car accidents. A pain management specialist's goal is to create a treatment plan that helps manage your pain so that you can return to normal as soon as possible without relying on long-term medication or surgery. Epidural steroid injections (ESIs) are one of the most common treatment options that pain management specialists offer for lower back and leg pain, which can help reduce inflammation and discomfort in your muscles and joints. Other types of injections include trigger point, facet, and nerve block.

ORTHOPEDIC SURGEON

Orthopedic surgeons specialize in the diagnosis and surgical treatment of injuries and illnesses involving the bones, joints, ligaments, tendons, and muscles. After a car crash, an orthopedic surgeon can treat broken bones, torn ligaments, and other damage to your joints.

Accidents can also trigger or aggrevate degenerative diseases, such as arthritis, sciatica, tendonitis, or spinal stenosis, and seeking treatment from an orthopedic surgeon can help you avoid developing these illnesses.

SPINE SPECIALIST

Spine specialists (usually spinal orthopedic surgeons or neurosurgeons) specialize in diagnosing and treating conditions of the spinal cord, spine, and nerves. Car accidents can damage any number of vertebrae or discs in your spinal column, resulting in pain or loss of sensation. A spine specialist can treat these injuries, as well as any other spinal damage the accident caused.

NEUROLOGIST OR NEUROSURGEON

Neurologists and neurosurgeons both diagnose and treat conditions affecting the brain and nervous system. However, while neurosurgeons specialize in operating on the brain and spinal cord, neurologists do not perform surgeries. You may want to seek treatment from a neurologist or neurosurgeon if you experience neurological issues such as headaches, migraines, or tingling, numbness, or weakness in your extremities after a car crash.

GENERAL SURGEON

General surgeons are medical doctors who have completed postgraduate surgical training. They attend to all types of general surgery cases, from abdominal and thoracic to head and neck injuries. They can diagnose and treat most car accident injuries that require surgical repair, such as internal organ damage that causes internal bleeding.

PLASTIC SURGEON

Plastic surgeons specialize in repairing and reconstructing parts of the body, including skin, bone, muscle, and tendons. This includes repairing facial injuries, restoring function, and fixing burns and scars after a car crash. A plastic surgeon can correct facial disfigurements by removing unsightly marks on the skin or even reconstructing facial structures, if necessary.

IMAGING EXAMS

If you have been injured in a car accident, your treating physician may order imaging exams to help them diagnose how badly you are hurt. These scans can help doctors identify the types of injuries you have sustained to determine what treatment you should receive.

Some of the most common types of imaging procedures include:
- X-rays for major bone fractures
- Magnetic resonance imaging (MRI) for soft tissue injuries
- Computed tomography (CAT) scan for blood clots, organ damage, and bone fractures

Chapter 15

Who Pays for Treatment?

The general rule is that you are solely responsible for paying your medical bills as they are incurred, even if the other driver was clearly at fault for the accident. You can be reimbursed when the settlement is reached.

You can do this in several different ways:

1. MEDPAY

Some drivers have medical payment insurance coverage (commonly known as "MedPay") through their auto insurance. The amount can be $1,000 to $10,000 or more.

Call your insurer for the full policy coverage sheet if you're unsure you have MedPay. The sheet shows if you have MedPay and, if you do, how much you have.

MedPay covers your medical bills as they incur, up to your policy limit. Once you hit this, you're responsible for covering the rest. For example, if you have $5,000 MedPay and your chiropractic bill is $6,000, then you would have to pay the remaining $1,000.

Most medical providers treating accident victims, such as chiropractors or spine doctors, will know how to use your MedPay benefits. They will ask for your insurance policy and claim numbers and seek MedPay directly from the insurance company. That way, you don't have to pay anything out of pocket.

Your auto insurance will most likely claim reimbursement when you use MedPay and later win a settlement that includes paid medical bills.

Most MedPay coverage also applies to passengers, so you may be able to use your or the driver's MedPay coverage if you were a passenger in an accident. Note that every insurance contract varies, so it's important to contact your insurance company to confirm the detailed terms.

2. HEALTH INSURANCE (PRIVATE, MEDI-CAL, MEDICARE)

Health insurance will cover your expenses according to your policy, so it's highly recommended that you use your health insurance if you have one. However, you will have to pay any co-pay or deductible.

Health Insurance Subrogation: Just like MedPay, your health insurance provider could demand reimbursement if you win a settlement that pays the medical bills.

3. LIEN-BASED TREATMENT

If you don't have health insurance or MedPay, then you may be able to arrange payment terms with your physician(s). Some medical providers will work on a lien basis, which means they forgo payment until you receive your settlement. A personal injury attorney representing you can connect you to healthcare providers willing to work on a lien basis. It may be hard to get treatment if you don't have an attorney.

4. PAY OUT-OF-POCKET

This simply means you cover your own expenses.

Chapter 16

Can You Get a Settlement for Your Injuries?

WHAT IS A SETTLEMENT?

A settlement agreement is essentially a mutually beneficial compromise between you and the insurance company.

After a motor vehicle crash, you are legally entitled to seek compensation for your injuries and financial losses by filing a lawsuit. However, the other driver's insurance company will usually offer you a settlement if you agree not to sue them because it will save them money to avoid litigation.

Accepting a reasonable settlement can benefit you because you can avoid the long and tedious process of going to court. Settlements also mean you avoid the risk of losing at trial, in which case you will receive zero compensation.

WHAT KIND OF DAMAGES ARE INCLUDED IN MY SETTLEMENT?

The damages available through an insurance settlement are generally the same as those you could recover in court. The damages you can recover for injuries include:

- Medical bills
- Lost wages
- Pain and suffering
- Loss of earning capacity
- Scarring and disfigurement

(Check out chapter 3 for a detailed description of each of these damage types).

CALCULATING AN INJURY SETTLEMENT

Calculating the value of a case is not a simple calculation; however, the following example could help you understand the basics of injury settlement.

Dan rear-ended Paul and was determined to be at fault. Paul went to the ER that night due to severe neck and back pain. He then saw his doctor a few days later, who recommended he undergo physical therapy, which he did so for ten weeks.

MEDICAL BILLS

- The ER visit was **$7,500**
- The doctor visit was **$700**
- Physical therapy was **$10,000**

Therefore, Paul's total medical expenses were **$18,200** ($7,500 + $700 + $10,000).

LOST WAGES

- Paul missed a total of **60 hours** of work due to his doctor visits.
- He earns **$30 per hour**.

Therefore, Paul's total lost wages were **$1,800** (60 x $30).

PAIN AND SUFFERING

Paul's pain and suffering damages were determined to be **$20,000** after negotiations.

TOTAL SETTLEMENT

Paul's total settlement would be **$40,000** ($18,200 + $1,800 + $20,000).

WHAT IF MY HEALTH INSURANCE COVERS MY BILLS?

The settlement includes medical bills already paid — by either you or your health insurance. However, your health insurance company may have the right to be reimbursed from the proceeds of the settlement.

IN SUMMARY

A settlement agreement is a mutually beneficial compromise between you and the insurance company. After a motor vehicle crash, you are legally entitled to seek compensation for your injuries and financial losses by filing a lawsuit; however, the other driver's insurance company will usually offer you a settlement if you agree not to sue them.

The types of damages you can recover after a car accident include:

- Medical bills
- Lost wages
- Pain and suffering
- Loss of earning capacity
- Scarring and disfigurement

Chapter 17

Documents Supporting Your Injury Claim

It is essential that you have solid documentation for all claimed damages. Insurance adjusters are required to provide evidence for every cent they pay out in a settlement. The more thorough the documentation you submit, the more likely you'll be able to receive quick and fair compensation. The insurance company likely won't pay you if you can't back up a claim with documents.

A law firm will collect all necessary records for you. Additionally, they will prepare a demand packet to send to the insurance companies and negotiate a settlement on your behalf. However, these are the essential documents you need to prepare a demand packet yourself if you don't have a lawyer.

If you are handling the claim yourself, "Winning Settlement Strategies," an online course created by Injury Claims 101, will teach you what you need to know to obtain the best possible settlement.

Below are the types of documentation you should keep and submit for each category of damages.

MEDICAL RECORDS AND BILLS

You will need both the bills themselves and copies of your medical records to receive compensation for your medical expenses. Make sure to request all medical records from the diagnosis and treatment of your injuries, including diagnostic images such as MRIs and x-rays. You'll also need to keep track of out-of-pocket expenses, such as prescriptions and transportation to and from appointments.

Your medical records will establish your injuries and identify their cause in most situations. This is crucial because you need documentation not only to show that you were injured, but that you were also injured in the car accident. It's common practice for insurance companies to argue that your injuries were caused by something other than the accident, so it's crucial that your documentation shows otherwise.

Obtaining medical records from larger hospitals and medical providers may take a few weeks or even months. You will often need to go through their records or billing departments and then wait for them to process your request. With smaller hospitals, chiropractors, or physical therapists, you can just call and request them to send you all your medical records and billing statements related to the accident.

LOST WAGES

If your injuries from the car accident cause you to miss work, whether for treatment or a recovery period, you can receive damages for wages you would have earned. Just like for medical bills, you'll need to submit documentation to support any claim you make for lost wages.

Some of the documents you can submit are:

- **Doctor's note**
  Make sure you obtain a letter from your doctor describing your injuries, the treatment you received, and the recovery process you need to heal. It should also explain why your injuries prevented you from working, as well as a recommendation for how much time to take off work.

- **Proof of pay rate**
  If you are a W-2 employee, the easiest way to prove your pay rate is by submitting your most recent pay stubs. If you don't have these, you can offer direct deposit records or the previous year's tax return or W-2. Those who are self-employed can submit business records, such as invoices for the same time of the prior year or the previous year's tax return, to establish how much money you would have made in the period you were unable to work.

- **Letter from your employer**
  If you're employed, you should also submit a letter from your employer (on company letterhead, if possible), verifying that you missed work. The letter should include your name, position, the days or hours you missed, your pay rate, and how many hours you work in each pay period.

PAIN AND SUFFERING

Pain and suffering damages are a large part of your claim. The physical and emotional pain you experience, and its effect on your quality of life, can entitle you to substantial compensation. You must thoroughly document what you are experiencing to ensure you are fairly reimbursed for your pain and suffering.

Don't trust your memory — the best way to record your physical and mental pain and suffering is to keep a journal detailing any:

- Pain or discomfort
- Confusion or difficulty remembering the accident
- Missed activities or changes in behavior
- Impact on relationships
- Emotional turmoil
- Humiliation
- Stress, anxiety, or restlessness
- Trouble sleeping

You can also use this journal to record any other impact your injuries have on your life. For example, are you unable to pick up or play with your child like you usually do? Did you have to hire a gardener or repair person to take care of jobs you typically would do yourself? Any time you do something differently because of your injury, document the occurrence in your journal.

OTHER DOCUMENTATION

Keep any receipts for out-of-pocket expenses caused by the injury, such as medications or hiring professionals to take care of tasks you would usually do yourself. Any time you spend money you usually would not have because of the injury, keep the receipt.

IN SUMMARY

You should keep the following types of documentation for each category of damages:

Medical bills: the bills themselves, plus copies of your medical records. Make sure to request ALL medical records from the diagnosis and treatment of your injuries, including diagnostic images such as MRIs and x-rays. You'll also need to keep track of out-of-pocket expenses like prescriptions and transport to and from appointments.

Lost wages: You can receive damages for wages if your injuries from the car accident cause you to miss work. Supporting documents you can submit are:

- Doctor's note
- Proof of pay rate
- Letter from your employer

Pain and suffering: commonly the large part of your claim. The physical and emotional pain you experience, and its effect on your quality of life, can entitle you to receive substantial compensation.

It's essential that you document what you are experiencing. Don't trust your memory — the best way is to keep a journal detailing the physical and mental impact your injuries have had on your life.

Other documentation: Receipts for any out-of-pocket expenses caused by the injury.

Chapter 18

Demand Letter

After collecting all the relevant medical records, your law firm will prepare a demand letter to send to the insurance adjuster.

This letter is the starting point for negotiations, making it one of the most critical steps in securing a full and fair insurance settlement.

As discussed in the last chapter, you can prepare a demand letter yourself if you don't have a lawyer.

Below is a brief overview of the demand letter's contents.

STATEMENT OF FACTS

Despite the insurance adjuster already being aware of the facts and circumstances involved in the car crash, you should describe the accident from your point of view. Not only does this tell the adjuster your side of the story, but it also gives an idea of what your testimony would be if you can't reach a settlement agreement and you go to trial.

You should specifically list the events leading up to and what happened during the accident. You should include the following details in your statement of facts:

- Accident date and location
- The direction both you and the other driver were heading
- Why the other driver is at fault

You can support your statement of facts, particularly the other driver's liability, with evidence, such as police reports, witness statements, and accident photos. A police report citing the other driver or identifying them as the at-fault party is strong proof that they are liable, so make sure to include this evidence if you have it.

INJURIES YOU SUSTAINED IN THE ACCIDENT AND ALL RESULTING MEDICAL TREATMENT

State the injuries you suffered due to the accident and all the medical treatment you received for those injuries. Start your list with any immediate pain or symptoms you experienced at the scene. Include any emergency medical services you received at the time and back this up with the paramedics' treatment report whenever possible.

Detail all medical treatment from the accident date until you stopped. Be sure to include your medical care providers' names and a summary of treatments received. It's also important to use medical terminology when describing the diagnoses and treatments you received.

Back up your claims with medical records and any correspondences with your medical providers.

MEDICAL EXPENSES

Include a detailed and comprehensive list of all medical costs related to treatment. You should count the full amount in your list of medical expenses, even if your health insurance paid the bill.

Additionally, make sure you include:
- Ambulance charges
- Prescription medication
- Medical devices, such as crutches or wheelchairs

LOST WAGES

Detail the amount of time you missed work because of your injury, as well as your income and the amount of money you would have earned when you were off work. Include any taken vacation time or paid time off (PTO) to stay home. If you are self-employed or have irregular employment, provide an explanation for how you calculated your lost wages.

PAIN AND SUFFERING

Describe the pain and suffering the accident caused.

This is where you use your journal. Choose entries that emphasize your pain and suffering the most and summarize them in your letter. For example, include whether you missed an important family event, such as a wedding or graduation. You should also detail specific activities you cannot perform due to your injuries.

This section should also detail emotional distress damages, such as anxiety, depression, or post-traumatic stress disorder (PTSD), if you have any. Just like a physical injury, you should support any emotional distress claims with documentation, such as medical records. For this reason, it's essential that you report your mental symptoms to your doctors at every appointment.

MONETARY DEMAND

State a demand for a dollar amount you'd be willing to accept to settle the case. This number should represent the total compensation you should receive for all your damages.

Since this is a negotiation, the number you start with will almost always be higher than the settlement you'll actually receive. Make sure you start high so that you can come down in the negotiation process and get the amount you actually want.

ATTACHMENTS

You'll need to attach supporting documentation, such as:
- Police reports and witness statements
- Medical records and bills
- Wage loss documents
- Any other substantiating evidence

TIPS FOR WRITING YOUR DEMAND LETTER

- Make sure your letter clearly details any facts about your claim that warrant a higher payout. Did you miss your son's graduation? Can you no longer participate in activities or hobbies you used to enjoy? Make sure your letter tells the insurance company about the adverse effects the accident has had on your life.

- Reread and edit your letter at least once to make sure it is error-free. Double-check all names, addresses, phone numbers, email addresses, and monetary amounts.

- Communicate the full extent of your injuries, but do not exaggerate. If the insurance company thinks you are lying about one thing, then it will make them suspicious about every aspect of your letter.

IN SUMMARY

- **Statement of facts**: Despite the insurance adjuster already being aware of the facts and circumstances involved in the car crash, you should start your letter by describing the accident from your point of view.

- **Injuries you sustained in the accident and all resulting medical treatment**: Detail ALL the injuries you suffered due to the accident and ALL the medical treatment you received for those injuries.

- **Medical expenses**: Include a detailed and comprehensive list of all your medical costs related to treatment.

- **Lost wages**: Detail the amount of time you missed work due to your injury, as well as your income and the amount of money you would have earned when you were off work.

- **Pain and suffering:** Describe the emotional distress and pain and suffering the accident caused. Provide the insurance company with detailed information about your pain and suffering — both physical and mental.

- **Monetary demand**: End the letter with a demand for a dollar amount you'd be willing to accept to settle the case. This number should represent the total compensation you should receive for all your damages.

Chapter 19

Negotiations

The negotiation process is conducted through written correspondence or phone calls. Your lawyer and the insurance adjuster will go back and forth and settle on a number somewhere between your lawyer's initial demand and the adjuster's initial offer.

This chapter will provide you with some guidance on how to negotiate your claim yourself if you do not have a lawyer.

WHEN WILL SETTLEMENT NEGOTIATIONS BEGIN?

Negotiations usually begin about a week or two after the insurance adjuster receives your demand letter. This time may vary depending on your claim's complexity and the adjuster's schedule.

The adjuster's counteroffer will almost always be low compared to the value of the possible damages and your demand.

NEGOTIATION TIPS

A few tips to help you when negotiating with the insurance company are below.

TIP #1: DON'T LET THE ADJUSTER THINK YOU'RE DESPERATE OR IN A HURRY TO SETTLE

If the insurance adjuster can sense that you are desperate to settle the claim or that you need cash ASAP, then they will use that to their advantage and offer you even less. Just try to be patient; you won't settle your accident claim in one day, and the sooner you accept this, the better you can negotiate.

Pace yourself and don't call the adjuster every day — give it a week or two. Even better, wait for the adjuster to contact you.

TIP #2: HAVE A SETTLEMENT AMOUNT IN MIND

You should determine the minimum amount you would be willing to accept before you talk to the adjuster about your demand. DO NOT SHARE THIS INFORMATION WITH THE ADJUSTER. Instead, just make sure to keep it in mind while negotiating.

You may need to adjust your minimum as negotiations progress. For example, increase your minimum amount if it matches the adjuster's first counteroffer since your claim is clearly worth more. On the other hand, if the adjuster has strong arguments about why your claim should be worth less, you may need to adjust downward to stay within a realistic range.

TIP #3: EMPHASIZE YOUR STRONGEST ARGUMENTS

You do not need to restate every fact — you did this in your demand letter. Instead, emphasize your strongest arguments.

You can also stress emotionally-powerful arguments in your favor. For example, if you could not care for or interact with your children the way you usually would, point out that the injury hurt both you and your family. While it's difficult to assign a specific dollar amount to your emotional distress and pain and suffering, this part of your claim is often the most valuable and can help you get a better offer.

TIP #4: PROVIDE EVIDENCE OF YOUR PAIN AND SUFFERING

As for all your other injuries, it helps to provide the insurance adjuster with some cold hard evidence showing that you experienced pain and suffering. Examples of documentation you can submit to prove this include:

- Medical records describing your pain
- Witness statements regarding your anguish at the crash scene
- The detailed journal you kept of your healing journey
- Doctor's restrictions that limited your activities

The more documentation you can provide, the easier it is for the adjuster to validate a larger settlement.

TIP # 5: REALIZE WHEN YOU'VE RECEIVED THE INSURANCE COMPANY'S BEST OFFER

While it's crucial not to accept an offer too early in the negotiation process, you also need to realize when you've received a final offer. An easy way to test if you're dealing with the best offer is to ask the adjuster if they can go any higher. You can always ask them to request supervisor authorization to make a higher offer; if the answer is "no" several times, then you've probably reached the limit. However, an answer such as, "I can't go any higher at the moment" indicates that you haven't received the final offer, and you could still get a higher one in later negotiations.

Once you receive a final offer, the next step is to decide if you want to accept it or reject it and file a personal injury lawsuit. You may prefer to just accept the final offer if it is within or at least close to your desired range; however, consider all your options if the amount is significantly lower than what you determined your claim was worth.

TO SUE OR NOT TO SUE?

While you may not want to accept a settlement that you think is too low, it's important to factor in the benefits of settling. First, taking the case to court is much riskier — if you go to trial, the jury could decide against you, and you could walk away with an even lower amount. Accepting a settlement also allows you to get your money much more quickly and avoid spending a lot of time and money on litigation.

Accepting the settlement may be your best course of action if the offer and demand are close or you're not likely to receive much more in court. If you do decide to file a suit, I highly recommend that you hire a personal injury lawyer.

IN SUMMARY

A typical negotiation process: Typical steps in settlement include a demand letter, where you ask for a higher award than what you expect to receive.

The negotiation process usually begins about a week or two after the insurance adjuster receives your demand letter.

TIPS WHEN NEGOTIATING:

1. Don't let the adjuster think you're desperate or in a hurry to settle
2. Have a settlement amount in mind
3. Emphasize your strongest arguments
4. Provide evidence of your pain and suffering
5. Realize when you've received the insurance company's best offer

TO SUE OR NOT TO SUE?

While you may not want to accept a settlement that you think is too low, you should factor in the benefits of settling. Taking the case to court is much riskier, while accepting a settlement allows you to get your money much more quickly and avoid spending a lot of time and money on litigation.

Chapter 20

What Happens After the Case Settles?

Congratulations, you've reached a settlement in your car crash case! Coming to an agreement with an insurance company is usually a huge relief — particularly when it feels like it has taken forever to get there. However, it's important to keep in mind that there are a few steps left in the process after your personal injury case settles. We'll discuss these steps in this chapter.

DEDUCTING COSTS FROM YOUR SETTLEMENT

After you agree on a settlement, certain expenses must be deducted from the total settlement amount before you receive your money. Costs that must be deducted from your award include:

- Legal fees (if you hired an attorney). Generally, your attorney fees will be a contingency amount ranging from 33% to 40% of your total settlement.

- Case costs (if you hired an attorney). You also will need to deduct certain costs incurred during the case, including postage, medical record fees, and copying costs.

- Medical liens. You will need to pay any healthcare providers that provided treatment on a lien basis for their services. If you hired an attorney, the attorney will negotiate the medical liens for you.

INSURANCE SUBROGATION

As with medical liens, your health and auto insurance providers can also place liens on your settlement to receive reimbursement (also known as "subrogation").

Once you receive a settlement, you'll usually need to pay back health insurance or MedPay if you used these to cover medical expenses.

THE "MADE WHOLE" DOCTRINE

Fortunately, in California, there is a limitation on when you have to pay an insurance provider back. According to the Made Whole Doctrine, you must be "made whole" from all the damages sustained from the accident before you are required to reimburse an insurance company.

Imagine, for example, you incurred $10,000 in medical bills and $15,000 in lost wages after an accident, and your health insurance policy covers $2,000 of your medical expenses. If you receive a $30,000 settlement for your accident, then you could be considered to have been "made whole," and your health insurance provider has the right to be reimbursed for the $2,000 they paid.

However, if you only receive a $20,000 settlement, which is less than the number of damages you incurred, then you have not been "made whole," and your health insurance company won't be entitled to subrogation for the $2,000 they spent on your medical bills.

It's important to note that your insurance contract could include legal language that invalidates the Made Whole Doctrine. Your attorney can review your policy and explain how the rule will apply in your case.

THE COMMON FUND DOCTRINE

The Common Fund Doctrine is a legal rule that applies when several parties have an interest in the awards from the same lawsuit. This rule exists to protect injured victims from being taken advantage of by insurance companies that don't help pay for attorney fees and then demand full subrogation.

When the Common Fund Doctrine applies, the insurance provider that did not contribute to obtaining the settlement (both your auto and health insurance) must reduce the amount of reimbursement they are entitled to receive by the attorney fees for that portion of the settlement. So, if the lawyer charged 33% overall, then the insurance provider's subrogation payment would also reduce by 33%.

NEGOTIATING FOR A LARGER TAKE-HOME SETTLEMENT

When you purchase an insurance policy, the agreement typically requires you to reimburse your insurance company if you receive a settlement. However, you or your accident lawyer can negotiate with them to ensure that you still receive fair compensation for your injuries by arguing that the Made Whole Doctrine and/or the Common Fund Doctrine apply. The less you have to reimburse the insurance companies, the more of your settlement you get to keep for yourself.

MOTORCYCLE ACCIDENTS, BICYCLE ACCIDENTS, PASSENGER ACCIDENTS, PEDESTRIAN ACCIDENTS, AND RIDESHARE ACCIDENTS

Chapter 21

Motorcycle Accidents

R iding a motorcycle can be far more dangerous than driving a car. In fact, motorcycle riders are consistently and statistically over-represented in fatal traffic accidents.

If you ride a motorcycle, you should be aware of California's laws regarding motorcycle-vehicle crashes. In this chapter, we'll explore some of the common causes of motorcycle accidents and ways to avoid injuries, along with some insurance issues you may encounter in owning and operating a motorcycle.

COMMON CAUSES OF MOTORCYCLE CRASHES

Many things can go wrong when riding a motorcycle that can lead to a collision with a motor vehicle. While every motorcycle accident is different, some of the most common mistakes drivers can make that lead to crashes include:

- Failing to see a motorcycle
- Making turns or lane changes without looking

- Speeding or driving recklessly
- Misjudging a motorcycle's location or speed
- Distracted or impaired driving

Both motorcyclists and drivers can be found to be at fault in a vehicle-motorcycle collision.

LANE-SPLITTING ACCIDENTS

Another common cause of motorcycle crashes is lane splitting, which is only legal in California. This is a maneuver where motorcyclists pass between vehicles when traffic stops or moves slowly.

A motorcyclist can be found at fault for this kind of accident if they ride unsafely by speeding or weaving in and out of traffic while splitting lanes. Likewise, drivers of other vehicles can be held liable if they hit a motorcycle rider who was splitting lanes safely.

INSURANCE ISSUES IN MOTORCYCLE CRASHES

California law requires motorcyclists to carry a motorcycle liability insurance policy, with bodily injury coverage of at least $15,000 per person and $30,000 per accident and property damage coverage of at least $5,000. If you are at fault for a crash, then the other party can file a claim against your motorcycle insurance — just like they would against your auto insurance in a car accident.

As a motorcyclist in a motor vehicle accident, you can file a personal injury claim against the liability insurance policy of the driver of the other vehicle if they are at fault for the collision. This process proceeds in the same way as if you were driving a car at the time of the crash.

PROTECTIVE GEAR AND APPAREL

Wearing appropriate protective gear and apparel when riding a motorcycle will significantly increase your chances of avoiding serious injury in an accident. The California Vehicle Code requires all motorcycle riders and passengers to wear a U.S. Department of Transportation (DOT)-compliant motorcycle safety helmet. Additionally, it is strongly suggested that passengers and riders alike wear face and/or eye protection and protective apparel, including:

- Leather or long-sleeved jackets made of reflective material
- Long, heavy pants
- Closed-toe boots that cover the ankle
- Full-fingered leather gloves

If you sustain a head or neck injury in a motorcycle accident and you were not wearing a helmet, then it will be challenging to receive a full reimbursement from the driver of the other vehicle — even if they are found to be at fault for the accident. Since California has imposed a mandatory helmet requirement, not wearing one makes you comparatively negligent in causing your injury.

You may be able to recover damages for a head or neck injury in this situation if you can prove that the injury would have occurred even if you had been wearing a helmet. However, if you can't prove this, then you can still receive compensation for other injuries and property damage if the accident was the other driver's fault.

Chapter 22

Bicycle Accidents

As bicycles are becoming an increasingly popular form of transportation in California, the prevalence of bicycle accidents has also risen. Whether to commute or just for recreation, bicyclists are often on the road with drivers and pedestrians. Unfortunately, this can lead to dangerous collisions between cars and bikes.

If you're a cyclist, it's essential to know what happens if you're involved in a crash with a motor vehicle. This chapter outlines a few details to help you navigate the aftermath of a bicycle accident and ensure you receive adequate compensation for your injuries.

WHO'S AT FAULT?

While you may think that a person driving a motor vehicle would automatically be liable for damages in a bicycle collision, this is not always the case. In some situations, the cyclist can be found at fault, while in many cases, both the driver and cyclist contribute to the accident. It all depends on which party (or parties) behaved negligently when the accident occurred.

A common contributing factor to liability is right of way. Generally, traffic lights and stop signs indicate who has the right of way in a particular situation — usually the person who has a green light or arrives at a stop sign first. However, if a driver and a bicyclist simultaneously stop at a stop sign, then the person to the right has priority.

Some other reasons that drivers and cyclists can be found liable for accidents include:

- Failing to signal
- Failing to use appropriate lighting at night
- Driving a vehicle in the bike lane, which are solely for bicyclists. A driver obstructing a bike lane would most likely be found liable.

As previously discussed, California's pure comparative fault laws allow damages to be apportioned according to each party's level of fault in causing the collision. So, as a cyclist, you may still be able to recover damages for your injuries, even if you are also partially to blame.

WHO WILL PAY FOR MY DAMAGES?

In most situations, somebody's auto insurance will cover the costs of your injuries. Whether your policy or the driver's will pay depends on the facts of the accident. If a motor vehicle driver is at fault in a collision with a cyclist, then the injured cyclist should be able to recover compensation from the driver's liability insurance.

However, if the driver is uninsured or underinsured, or if you're injured in a hit-and-run accident, then you can't be reimbursed through the driver's liability policy. Fortunately, you can recover compensation through Uninsured Motorist coverage from your auto insurance provider, if you've purchased it. Your MedPay coverage can also be used to cover your medical expenses.

You could also receive payment for property damage and/or bodily injuries caused by a third party if you carry homeowner's or renter's insurance. Coverages vary among insurance providers, so you'll need to carefully review your policy to determine if you can be reimbursed for your bike accident. A personal injury attorney can also help you figure out the ,.. best way to pursue damages after a bicycle-car accident.

Chapter 23

Passenger Accidents

So far in this book, we have focused on motor vehicle drivers who are involved in car accidents. But what about passengers? In nearly every situation, the driver of at least one vehicle involved in the accident is at fault — it is seldom the passenger. As a passenger in a car crash, you are also eligible for compensation for your injuries.

WHO IS LIABLE FOR A PASSENGER'S INJURIES?

In general, the injured passenger can file a personal injury insurance claim against whichever party is found to be at fault for the accident. It does not matter which vehicle you were riding in — whoever is at fault will be held responsible, whether it was the person driving you or the other car. If a car you are riding in is involved in a single-vehicle accident, then that driver will usually be considered completely at fault.

WHAT IF A FAMILY MEMBER IS AT FAULT?

There's an important caveat to keep in mind. Say you are riding in a vehicle, and your spouse is driving. The accident would be your spouse's fault, so you probably won't be able to file a claim against your spouse's policy. This is because family members you live with, such as your spouse or child, are generally considered to be insured people under most auto insurance policies. This means that you are barred from making a liability claim against your own policy.

Liability can become a little more complicated when multiple drivers are found to have contributed to the accident. For example, say Anna and Beth were driving vehicles and were involved in an accident. Cassie was a passenger in Anna's car. If Anna was found to be 30% at fault for the collision and Beth was 70% liable, then Cassie would be able to pursue proportional compensation from both drivers. So, if Cassie had $10,000 worth of damages, Anna would be responsible for $3,000, and Beth $7,000.

DO PASSENGERS NEED A PERSONAL INJURY LAWYER?

While passengers generally do not have to worry about insurance companies blaming them for the accident, adjusters will still resort to the same old tricks to attempt to diminish your claim's value. For example, they may try to minimize the severity of your injuries or argue that the accident did not cause them. Having a personal injury attorney negotiate with the insurance companies can help you maximize your settlement.

Additionally, just because the insurance company probably won't blame you for the accident doesn't mean they won't try to shirk responsibility. Injured passengers commonly face situations where the drivers' insurance providers disagree over who is responsible for the accident. It's easy for a passenger's rights to be pushed to the backburner during such disputes, so you should consider pursuing legal representation to ensure you are not forgotten.

Chapter 24

Pedestrian Accidents

Whether walking to the grocery store or crossing a busy street, being on foot can be more dangerous than you think. Injuries can be severe when a motor vehicle hits a pedestrian, particularly if the car was traveling at high speed.

When you are injured in a pedestrian accident, you may be able to receive a settlement or other form of financial relief for your injuries by filing a personal injury claim against the driver's liability insurance policy. If you have been injured in a pedestrian accident, it's highly recommended that you hire a personal injury lawyer since your injuires are likely severe.

IS THE DRIVER ALWAYS AT FAULT?

Although the driver is usually at fault in a pedestrian car accident, pedestrians can also be found partially or even fully liable. Contrary to popular belief, pedestrians do not always have the right of way, and in some situations, they may be at fault (or partially at fault) for a crash.

Motor vehicle drivers have a legal obligation to exercise additional caution in locations where pedestrians are or are likely to be present, such as an intersection. Similarly, pedestrians have a legal duty to use reasonable care when crossing a street.

LIABILITY ISSUES IN PEDESTRIAN ACCIDENTS

Some specific laws from the California Vehicle Code that apply to fault in vehicle-pedestrian accidents include the following:

- Pedestrians are not permitted to jaywalk under any circumstances.
- Vehicles are required to yield the right of way to pedestrians who are crossing a crosswalk at an intersection.
- Vehicles are not permitted to stop inside a crosswalk.
- Vehicles are not permitted to pass other vehicles stopped at a crosswalk.
- Vehicles are not permitted on sidewalks except for garage and alley entrances and exits — even in these situations, drivers must yield to pedestrians using the sidewalk.

Additionally, when a pedestrian acts in such a way that it is impossible for a motorist who is driving in a normal, cautious manner to avoid hitting them, then the pedestrian will be found at fault. For example, if a pedestrian causes the collision by jumping directly in front of a vehicle matching the speed limit, then the pedestrian will be found liable for the accident.

DOES AUTO INSURANCE COVER PEDESTRIAN ACCIDENT INJURIES?

Pedestrians can file a personal injury claim against a driver's auto insurance policy when the driver is found to be at fault.

The process would then proceed similarly to the claim-filing process in a two-vehicle accident.

If the driver is uninsured or underinsured, then the pedestrian can receive compensation from their Uninsured Motorist (UM) or Underinsured Motorist (UIM) policy, if they have one. The pedestrian's MedPay coverage can also be used to cover their medical expenses when the driver doesn't have insurance. First-party UM/UIM and MedPay insurance can also be used to reimburse the pedestrian in the case of a hit-and-run accident.

Chapter 25

Rideshare Accidents

Rideshare services, such as Uber and Lyft, can be a great way to get around in California, but who is responsible for your injuries if you get into an accident? What if a rideshare driver hits your vehicle? Liability issues in rideshare accidents are a little more complicated than other types of car crashes, so it's essential to understand the answers to these questions before catching a ride.

WHAT HAPPENS IF I GET INTO AN ACCIDENT WHILE RIDING IN AN UBER OR LYFT?

California law categorizes rideshare corporations, such as Uber and Lyft, as "transportation network companies," also known as TNCs. California law also requires that TNCs carry a minimum of $1 million in both commercial liability and Uninsured/Underinsured Motorist (UM/UIM) insurance.

So, if your Uber or Lyft driver causes an accident, then the rideshare company's liability insurance will usually cover your damages as an injured passenger if the driver was at fault.

However, if the other driver is at fault, you should pursue a claim against the other driver's liability insurance, just like you would as a passenger in a non-rideshare vehicle. If the at-fault driver does not have insurance or is underinsured, then the rideshare company's UM/UIM policy would typically reimburse you for your injuries.

WHICH INSURANCE COVERAGE APPLIES IF A RIDESHARE DRIVER HITS ME?

If you are driving or riding in a vehicle involved in an accident caused by an Uber or Lyft driver, then you can pursue a claim against them. However, liability for your injuries will depend on the rideshare driver's status at the time of the accident.

The driver's status can fall into three different categories:

- Driving with the app off and with no passenger
- Waiting for a trip assignment with the app on
- Actively driving a passenger or en route to pick one up

The applicable insurance coverage will vary based on which category applies to the driver when the crash occurred.

DRIVING WITH THE APP OFF AND WITH NO PASSENGER

If the Uber or Lyft driver did not have the app on when the accident occurred, then the crash is considered to have happened outside the scope of their rideshare services. This means that it will be treated just like a regular car crash, and the driver's personal liability insurance will be responsible.

WAITING FOR A TRIP ASSIGNMENT WITH THE APP ON

If the Lyft or Uber driver had the app on and was waiting for a ride to be assigned at the time of the crash, then the rideshare company's contingent coverage should kick in. California law requires minimum contingent coverage of $50,000 per person, $100,000 per accident, and $30,000 in property damage.

ACTIVELY DRIVING A PASSENGER OR EN ROUTE TO PICK ONE UP

If the accident occurred while the Uber or Lyft driver is carrying a passenger or they have accepted a trip and are on the way to pick up the fare, then the rideshare company's $1 million commercial liability policy would be responsible.

Made in the USA
Las Vegas, NV
27 January 2023

66203829R10097